WHAT ARE THEY SAYING ABOUT MARK?

What Are They Saying About Mark?

Daniel J. Harrington, SJ

PAULIST PRESS
New York/Mahwah, N.J.

Cover design by James Brisson
Book design by Theresa M. Sparacio

Library of Congress Cataloging-in-Publication Data

Harrington, Daniel J.
    What are they saying about Mark? / Daniel J. Harrington.
      p. cm.
    Includes bibliographical references.
    ISBN 0-8091-4263-5 (alk. paper)
    1. Bible. N.T. Mark—Criticism, interpretation, etc. I. Title.

BS2585.52.H37 2005
226.3'07—dc22

                                   2004015172

Published by Paulist Press
997 Macarthur Boulevard
Mahwah, New Jersey 07430

www.paulistpress.com

Printed and bound in the
United States of America

Contents

1
Introduction:
Looking Backward and Forward

Perhaps the most striking development in biblical studies in recent years has been the proliferation of methods used in approaching the texts. While at least in some circles the historical-critical method remains fundamental, biblical interpreters now routinely draw upon "new" approaches developed in linguistics, literary studies, and the social sciences.

So pervasive and prominent has this development been that in 1993 the **Pontifical Biblical Commission** published an excellent guide to the strengths and weaknesses of these various methods. The document is entitled *The Interpretation of the Bible in the Church* (1993). Issued with full papal approval, it has been received positively and enthusiastically not only by Catholics but also by Protestant and Jewish biblical scholars.

Prepared by an international team of distinguished Catholic biblical scholars, this document describes the various methods of and approaches to biblical interpretation, examines certain hermeneutical questions, reflects on the characteristic features of a Catholic interpretation of the Bible, and considers the place of biblical interpretation in the life of the church. It spells out in detail many of the directions recommended in earlier papal encyclicals and in Vatican II's Constitution on Divine Revelation *(Dei verbum).* While calling historical-criticism "an indispensable method for the scientific study of the meaning of ancient texts," the document gives ample attention to the possible contributions of "new" literary and social-scientific methods, criticizes fundamentalism as a danger and even an invitation to "a kind of intellectual suicide," and insists on the pastoral significance of the entire exegetical enterprise.

In many cases an important testing ground for the application of these new methods for biblical interpretation has been the Gospel of Mark. As a fast-moving and sophisticated narrative about Jesus' public ministry issuing in his passion and death, Mark's Gospel lends itself to literary analysis. As a story set in the land of Israel around 30 CE, but written down around 70 CE either in Rome, Galilee, or southern Syria, Mark's Gospel is a text that needs illumination by ancient parallel texts and by the detective work that historians customarily perform. And as a religious writing about Jesus as God's agent and his proclamation of the kingdom of God, Mark's Gospel raises questions and provides direction for theologians and indeed for all who are interested in ultimate realities and in ancient and present-day religious and political struggles.

This volume carries forward the project begun by Frank J. Matera in his similarly titled *What Are They Saying About Mark?* (1987, now out of print). The five chapters in his work dealt with the setting of Mark's Gospel, its Christology, its treatment of Jesus' disciples, its composition, and its narrative. While Matera's focus was on Markan scholarship between the early 1960s and 1985, he also took the occasion to set forth some general information about Mark's Gospel. All of these matters are treated in this volume, but now in a somewhat different framework that corresponds to what has taken place in Markan studies since that time.

My framework seeks especially to accommodate the many attempts at applying the "new" methods to the study of Mark's Gospel. In the second chapter the starting point is how Mark's Gospel has been approached from different angles according to the perspectives of modern literary criticism. The third chapter examines how the major theological topics—Christology, the use of the Old Testament, discipleship, community life, and faith and related themes — that emerge from literary study of this Gospel have been treated. The fourth chapter explores efforts at clarifying the historical setting of the Gospel's composition and the materials that might have been available to the Evangelist as he put them into narrative form. The fifth chapter concerns the "engaged" — feminist, political, and pastoral — readings that the Gospel has generated in recent years, and describes a few commentaries that synthesize and reflect directions in recent Markan studies. The bibliography provides full bibliographical information about the books and articles treated in the main text.

Biblical exegesis is a literary, historical, and theological discipline. But since these are not entirely separate operations, the chapter divisions are admittedly somewhat artificial. Indeed, a major theme in this book is to show how the various methods work together in interpreting Mark's Gospel. The theological and historical studies involve literary analysis. And the literary studies enter into the concerns of history and frequently supply the groundwork for theological conclusions. The so-called engaged readings, while looking toward the meaning of Mark in the present, naturally depend on literary, historical, and theological analysis. I have placed the various publications in the category and subcategory where I judge their major thrust is, and treated them according to the chronological order of their publication. At the end of each chapter I take stock of what has been accomplished and suggest some ways forward (and backward).

What follows is primarily an objective report on some important books and articles about Mark's Gospel (all but one in English) that have been published since 1985, where Frank Matera's survey left off. My focus is mainly on what "they" (that is, reputable biblical scholars) have been saying about Mark's Gospel over the last twenty or so years. At the end of each chapter I follow Matera's example and offer my own brief reflections on the issues under discussion and make known my own views and judgments. Since this kind of book is intended primarily for New

Testament scholars, theologians, students, and pastors, I have stressed studies that are of general significance rather than entering into debate regarding matters of exegetical details.

For what I think about Mark's Gospel in general and about each passage in it, the reader may consult the large commentary that I co-authored with John R. Donahue in the Sacra Pagina series under the title *The Gospel of Mark* (2002). In the introduction to that commentary I expressed regret that we offered relatively little explicit interaction with the views of other scholars. The invitation to write this little book on Markan studies since 1985 has made it possible for me to fill what I acknowledged to be a lacuna in our work. At the same time my rereading of the works of other scholars after completing our commentary has occasionally made me wish that I could now add to our work some of their observations on particular passages.

As a way of showing where Markan studies were around 1985, I will first present a summary of Frank Matera's contribution to the What Are They Saying About... series. I regard Matera's work as a perceptive, fair, and balanced picture of Markan research at the beginning of the period covered in this sequel, and I agree with most of his views (though I think that this Gospel is more "Jewish" than he seems to think). As a way of showing where Markan studies have been going, I will also describe a collection of essays developed early in the period considered in this book that can help in understanding why and how Markan research has moved in the ways it has. These two books show where Markan studies were around 1985 and where they have been going ever since.

Looking Backward

With regard to the setting in which Mark's Gospel was composed, Matera reviewed the arguments about its place and date. Those like Martin Hengel who defended the traditional Roman provenance had on their side a large dossier of patristic references going back to Papias. Those who argued for the Gospel's origin in Galilee (Willi Marxsen, Werner Kelber) or in southern Syria (Howard Clark Kee) built their cases mainly on internal evidence in the text, especially in Mark 13. While almost everyone agreed that Mark's Gospel was composed around 70 CE, opinions were divided over whether it was shortly before or shortly after the destruction of Jerusalem and its temple in 70 CE. At the end of each chapter Matera expressed his own opinions. On the topic of setting he wrote: "In my view the setting for Mark's Gospel is a predominantly Gentile community, threatened by persecution, excited by apocalyptic speculation, and forgetful of the cross. The Roman community of the late 60s, a recent victim of Nero's persecution and now fearful of the outcome of the Jewish war, is a likely candidate" (p. 17).

In his survey of developments in the study of Mark's Christology, Matera took as his starting point William Wrede's theory of the "messianic secret" and noted that scholars agreed on little more than the proposition that the secret of Jesus' identity cannot be understood apart from the cross. He also described the different attempts by Theodore Weeden and Norman Perrin in the late 1960s and the early 1970s to show that Mark sought to correct a false "divine man"/"theology of glory" Christology that was threatening Mark's community. But the evanescence of the "divine man" *(theios anēr)* figure supposedly being promoted by Mark's opponents caused these proposals to lose favor among Markan scholars to the point that they now are regarded as historical curiosities.

The more substantive and lasting debate among scholars were related to Mark's use of the three most prominent christological titles in his narrative about Jesus: Messiah, Son of God, and Son of Man. While some sought to find tensions among these three titles, more extensive treatments by Matera and other scholars revealed instead a confluence among them. Matera concluded that in Mark's high Christology Jesus was the long-awaited royal

Messiah; the paradox was that Jesus the Son of God and Son of Man fulfilled his messianic role as the crucified Messiah.

In the period covered by Matera, Mark's presentation of Jesus' disciples was interpreted in two different ways. The "polemical" interpretation viewed the disciples as representatives of the Jerusalem church opposed to the Gentile mission and as supporters of "false" theological positions about Christology, ecclesiology, or eschatology. The "pastoral" approach took Mark's portrayal of Jesus' disciples as aimed at building up his readers as Christians and showing them what true discipleship is (even by way of the disciples' at times negative example). Within the group of Jesus' disciples the Twelve seem to form an inner circle as they accompany Jesus and share in his mission. The chief Markan images for the church (according to Ernest Best) include the flock, temple, ship, community of knowledge, and house/household. By way of conclusion Matera expressed his preference for the "pastoral" approach, and noted that the "polemical" approach stands or falls with the "divine man" Christology.

This same period witnessed a remarkable shift in treating the composition of Mark's Gospel. Under the influence of form criticism, scholars in the 1960s and 1970s sought to isolate the various sources or collections used by Mark in the hope of clarifying Mark's own editorial or redactional contributions. But failure to reach consensus about Mark's sources led to a shift toward exploring Mark's own literary skill as shown, for example, in the controversies described in Mark 2:1–3:6, the parables in 4:1–34, and the doublets in 4:35–8:26. Even the passion narrative, long regarded as consisting mainly of very early pre-Markan tradition, came to be viewed as a vehicle for Mark's literary skill and ability as a creative theologian. Matera observed that the deadlock in the debate over whether Mark was a conservative redactor or a creative redactor led to a new focus on Mark as an author and theologian and on his Gospel as a literary work in its own right.

Matera wrote at a time (the mid-1980s) when the attention of Markan specialists had begun to turn to the narrative of the Gospel; that is, to the literary world created by the story of Jesus in the Gospel text. One literary approach focused on the alleged similarities of Mark's Gospel to ancient Greco-Roman tragedies, rhetoric, and biographies of disciple-gathering teachers. A second (and more fruitful) literary approach looked at Mark's Gospel with the questions and concerns of modern literary criticism. This approach considered how Mark's story is told (rhetorical devices) and what his narrative is about (setting, plot, characters). Matera concluded that it "may well be true that the most profitable agenda for Markan studies lies in the direction set by literary criticism" (p. 91). But he also cautioned against "the danger of dislodging the Gospel from its historical moorings" (p. 92).

Looking Forward

Perhaps the most important development in Markan studies over the past twenty years has been the shift in emphasis from the world behind the text (history, sources, etc.) to the text itself and to the reader of the text. For most of the twentieth century the focus in Markan research was on the person of Jesus (Mark as an entry point for recovering the historical Jesus), on the sources collected and used by the Evangelist Mark (form criticism as a literary and historical tool), and on the life and times of the Markan community (redaction criticism); however, in recent times there has developed a greater concentration on how the form of Mark's text that is available now to us communicates and on how it has been read in the past and is read today.

A good introduction to this shift in focus can be found in the collection entitled *Mark & Method: New Approaches in Biblical Studies,* edited by **Janice Capel Anderson** and **Stephen D. Moore** (1992). After Anderson's sketch of the various ways in which the Evangelist has been understood throughout the ages (as

Peter's scribe, an instrument of the Holy Spirit, a reliable chronicler, the front for an anonymous Christian community, etc.), she notes that Mark is now viewed mainly as a narrative thinker and theologian. Then five essays describe and illustrate with reference to Mark some of the new methods of approaching the Gospels.

First, Elizabeth Struthers Malbon explains that narrative criticism is chiefly concerned with the question, How does the story mean? She treats the major interests of narrative criticism (implied author and implied reader, characters, settings, and plot) and the rhetorical devices (repetition, intercalation, framing, foreshadowing, echoing, symbolism, and irony) that Mark calls upon to shape his story of Jesus.

The essay by Robert M. Fowler concerns reader-response criticism. This approach moves more explicitly to the reader and to the question, What or who determines the meaning of Mark? After reflecting on what goes into a reading of Mark's Gospel, he calls attention to features in the text that may elicit certain reactions or responses from the reader: devices that make us look forward and/or look back, that cause us to fill in narrative gaps, that force us to confront the possibility of irony, that may surprise us (the self-consuming narrative), or that may arouse resistance from the careful reader.

According to Stephen D. Moore in his essay on deconstructive criticism, Mark's Gospel is at least as close to the language of the unconscious (dreams, puns, etc.) as it is to the theological treatise or scholarly commentary. Using insights from Sigmund Freud and Jacques Derrida, Moore shows how deconstruction reads Mark "with an eye and ear extended for the excluded, the marginal, the blind spot, the blank" (p. 86).

In her essay on feminist criticism, Janice Capel Anderson first explains both feminist critique (uncovering the androcentric and patriarchal character of the Bible and of biblical scholarship, as well as passages that have been used to oppress women) and feminist construction (attending to female images of God and female figures in the Bible, reconstructing the historical and sociological background, recovering the history of women interpreting the Bible, and asking how gender shapes biblical interpretation). Then with a focus on the account of "the dancing daughter" in Mark 6:14–29, she reflects on how Herodias and her daughter have been negatively interpreted, chiefly by men, and introduces the approach of intertextuality by reading that passage in light of the Old Testament narratives about Esther, Judith, and Jezebel.

Under the heading of "social criticism," David Rhoads explains and illustrates four different operations with reference to the dynamics of clean and unclean in Mark's Gospel: (1) social description concerns the customs, laws, and practices related to pollution and purity in first-century Palestine; (2) social history examines how the sociopolitical history of the time shaped Mark's Gospel; (3) the sociology of knowledge explores the assumptions and worldview behind Mark's Gospel, and how they might provide clues to the social group behind it; and (4) social-science models deal with such matters as kinship systems, power relations, rituals, purity and pollution rules, economics, and so forth. These models can clarify the different attitudes toward purity and boundaries evident in Mark's Gospel.

Conclusion

Matera's survey covered a very lively and rich period in the history of Markan studies (1960–85). While some issues have faded away (such as the "divine man" Christology) and others continue to be contested (Rome or Syria-Palestine as the place of composition), the trends toward literary criticism and toward regarding Mark as an author and theologian in his own right have become more evident and even dominant. The "new" methods — narrative, reader-response, deconstructionist, feminist, and social — have taken their places in the "toolbox" of Markan research and become part of mainstream scholarship, as the chapters that follow will show.

2
Literary Studies

Literary analysis is basic to biblical study. To understand a Gospel text, we need to consider the context, the words and images, the characters, the structure or plot, the genre, and the content or message. Recent literary studies of Mark's Gospel have given special attention to the dynamics of reading and the effects that the text might have on its readers, how the parameters of space and time in which the narrative unfolds are set up, how various characters are portrayed and how they interact especially with Jesus as the main character, and what kind of text Mark's Gospel is and what it most resembles among the genres used in antiquity.

Literary Analysis

A good example of the new literary approach presented in a straightforward and highly accessible manner is **Bas van Iersel's** *Reading Mark* (1988). His point of departure is the observation that since Mark has been transmitted as a book that forms a unity, it can only be understood by someone who reads it in its entirety and tries to apprehend it as a meaningful whole. He proposes to read the Gospel primarily at the level of the implied author and the implied reader.

Taking Mark 1:1 as the title for the book, van Iersel perceives a concentric structure in the book as a whole:

> A1—in the desert (1:2–13)
> B1—in Galilee (1:16—8:21)
> C—on the way (8:27—10:45)
> B2—in Jerusalem (11:1–15:39)
> A2—at the tomb (15:42—16:8)

He takes 1:14–15 and 15:40–41 as "hinges," and gives particular prominence to the structural significance of the two giving-of-sight stories in 8:22–26 and 10:46–52.

In his expositions of the individual (large) sections, van Iersel works primarily at the level of literary analysis, incorporating methods such as structuralism, narrative analysis, and reader-response criticism (while carefully avoiding technical terms and academic jargon). For example, in dealing with Mark 1:1–15, which he entitles "Setting the Scene," he considers context, structure, times, places, and persons, as well as the content of the various subsections and their functions in Mark's story. His observations show how "after reading just one page of Mark the reader has become an initiate, already knowing much more than most characters will ever get to know in the course of the story" (p. 42).

Likewise in treating the Markan passion narrative (14:1—15:39) under the heading of "Elimination," van Iersel discusses context, structure, times, places, the various characters (adversaries, Pilate and his soldiers, supporters, Peter, the crowd and the individual, and Jesus), as well as the content of the specific episodes, and the key biblical texts in the background (Isa 52:13—53:12; Ps 22; Wis 2:12–20). The various elements in the Markan passion narrative serve to reveal at last the secret of Jesus' identity, which van Iersel describes in the following way: "The names used to explain who Jesus is cannot give a complete picture of his person and work unless it is clearly stated that this messiah and son of God eventually allowed his body to be broken and his blood to be shed by those who had given the highest priority to his violent death" (p. 196).

Reader-Response Criticism

In *Mark's Audience: The Literary and Social Setting of Mark 4.11–12* (1989), **Mary Ann Beavis** describes her perspective as "reader-response" analysis. She is especially concerned with how a Gospel that takes Isaiah 6:9–10 (= Mark 4:12) as its thematic principle might have been received by its original audience within the context of Greco-Roman education and culture. She contends that Mark's Gospel would have been used to convey information about Jesus not only to persons who were already Christians but also to "outsiders" who might be persuaded to inquire further into Jesus and his "mystery" of God's kingdom.

The most enigmatic and (even notorious) verses in Mark's Gospel appear in 4:11–12, between the parable of the sower and its explanation:

> 11. And he said to them, "To you has been given the secret of the kingdom of God, but for those outside, everything comes in parables; 12. in order that
> 'they may indeed look, but not perceive,
> and may indeed listen, but not understand;
> so that they may not turn again and be forgiven.'"

These verses contain several "objectionable" ideas. They suggest that Jesus distinguished between "insiders" and "outsiders," that he gave private explanations of his teaching ("the mystery of the kingdom of God") to some but not to others, and that the parables are deliberately obscure riddles that Jesus used in order to confound outsiders and prevent them from repenting.

Most modern interpreters regard these verses as either a garbled version of something that Jesus might have said and/or as an alien element intruded into the text of the Gospel. However, Beavis contends that Mark 4:11–12 introduces and crystallizes several important Markan themes (perception, comprehension, private teaching), and that the passage served a rhetorical and propagandistic function with respect to the original audience in that it invited the hearers to be party to "the mystery of the kingdom of God," the imminent Parousia of the Son of Man, by seeing, hearing, and understanding the Gospel's theology.

The Evangelist appears to have been a Christian scholar and missionary, possibly of Jewish extraction, with some training in Greek. In fact, Beavis maintains, the original audience would have perceived Mark's story of Jesus along the lines of a Greek tragedy with alternating sections of narrative and teaching (= chorus). And this audience would have been very familiar with the literary form of the *chreia* (a short narrative issuing in a decisive saying) that constitutes a large part of Mark's Gospel. In Beavis's reader-response perspective the apparently enigmatic Mark 4:11–12 is the hermeneutical key that opens up the entire Gospel.

In *Let the Reader Understand: Reader-Response Criticism and the Gospel of Mark* (1991), **Robert M. Fowler** set out to write a book not about the Gospel of Mark but rather about the *experience* of reading the Gospel of Mark. His focus is not so much what the Gospel says about Jesus as how it says it and the effects or impact that its mode of discourse has upon the reader. The basic thesis of the work is neatly summarized in the following statement: "Mark's Gospel is designed to guide, direct, and illuminate the reader vigorously and authoritatively, but at the same time challenge, puzzle, and humble its reader. It pulls the reader strongly in opposite directions simultaneously" (p. 220).

In the first part of his work Fowler explains the basic concepts of reader-response criticism. He argues that Mark's primary aim, like that of most good storytellers, is to persuade or somehow affect the reader. After distinguishing between the (mainly passive and accepting) reader and the (active and questioning) critic, he explains the "cast of characters" within the reading process: real author, implied author, narrator, narratee, implied reader, and real reader. For analyzing Mark's Gospel the most important figures are the implied author and the implied reader. Fowler also stresses that reading a narrative text like Mark's Gospel is a temporal experience (in which the reader changes over time) and is intended to construct the reader's response and achieve communion with its audience by means of a forceful event that takes place through time.

In the second part Fowler applies the methods and concerns of reader-response criticism to Mark's Gospel. He describes the Gospel's construction in this way: "The implied author puts forth a reliable, authoritative narrator, who puts forth a reliable, authoritative protagonist named Jesus" (p. 61). The narrator is predisposed to claim absolute authority, and the narratee is inclined to grant it. And the Gospel's primary goal is to affect the reader, not simply to pile up information about Jesus and his disciples.

This goal is achieved most obviously by the narrator's explicit commentary. Scattered throughout the Gospel there are parenthetical comments (e.g., 13:14), a title (1:1), an epigraph (1:2–3), various explanations (introduced by "for," "because," etc.), awkward syntax that forces the reader to think, and inside views (perceptions, emotions, knowledge, motivation, and interior or private speech).

The implicit commentary by the narrator is conveyed first of all by the characters (especially Jesus the protagonist) and by the plotting (paratactic-episodic narration, duality, open-ended narrative). There are also many instances of what Fowler calls the rhetorical strategies of indirection (irony, metaphor, paradox, ambiguity, and opacity) that the Markan narrator uses to shape the reading experience: "For the reader of Mark's Gospel Jesus is the experience of reading Mark's Gospel, and reading Mark's Gospel is experiencing Jesus" (p. 190).

From Fowler's analysis of how Mark's Gospel achieves its effect on the reader, the Evangelist emerges as something of a creative literary genius. He has skillfully defined the story and the character of Jesus through a rhetoric that is "powerfully, insistently direct *and* tantalizingly, intriguingly indirect" (p. 261). However, the result is an ambivalent narrative "that pulls (and entices) the reader vigorously (and seductively) in different directions simultaneously."

Nevertheless, many of us find it difficult to live with ambivalence. And Matthew, Luke, and John were no exceptions. Fowler shows how Matthew deliberately resolved many ambivalences and filled in many gaps that he found in Mark's Gospel. The result is that most readers both throughout the centuries and today tend to read Mark through Matthean spectacles (or reading grid), and so fail to appreciate the distinctive literary artistry and rhetorical effect of Mark's Gospel.

Using literary criticism combined with insights from the sociology of knowledge, **Jerry Camery-Hoggatt** in *Irony in Mark's Gospel: Text and Subtext* (1992) shows that irony is an integral factor in Mark's strategy of composition, and that it serves both apologetic and paradigmatic purposes. Camery-Hoggatt's basic insight is that irony not only is a property resident within the text but is also somehow resident in the reaction of the reader. In his use of irony Mark sets up an alliance among himself, the figure of Jesus, and the reader. They all possess essential knowledge that the human characters in the narrative do not have.

The strength of Camery-Hoggatt's work is that it explores in depth one literary device that is recurrent in the text and gives it literary unity. He also illustrates how the irony draws the reader into a relationship with the writer and evokes responses from the reader, and so both shatters old assumptions about the reader's social world and helps to build a new worldview for the reader.

A classic instance of Markan irony appears in the account of the Roman soldiers' mockery of Jesus in 15:16–20. Within the text the soldiers use the regalia of kings and emperors (purple cloak, crown of thorns, "Hail" as an invocation, a reed as scepter, etc.) to mock Jesus as King of the Jews/Messiah. Thus as characters in the narrative, the soldiers appear to be using irony among themselves vis-à-vis Jesus to display their allegedly superior knowledge that Jesus is not a king or a messiah. They make an ironic commentary on the popular identifications of Jesus as the Messiah/King of the Jews. But the joke is on them! The Evangelist and the reader are "in" on the reality that Jesus *is* the Messiah and King of the Jews. The soldiers' irony is trumped by the superior knowledge shared by the Evangelist and the reader. That irony evokes from the reader a further identification with the suffering and misunderstood Jesus and increases the reader's distance from Jesus' opponents and persecutors.

According to Camery-Hoggatt, Mark's use of irony has both social and literary functions. On the social level the use of irony forces the reader to raise questions concerning established assumptions about reality, thus envisioning the shattering of a social world (sociology of knowledge). In the concrete circumstances of the Gospel's composition "Mark's ironies express a crisis of loyalties between Christianity and traditional Judaism, at every point along the way calling into question those institutions and attitudes which oppose the emergence of this new and different expression of piety" (p. 180).

On the literary level, the device of irony runs through the Markan narrative from start to finish. The prologue (1:1–15) supplies the reader with essential knowledge that the human characters in the narrative (apart from Jesus) do not possess. Mark lets us know in 1:1 that Jesus is the Christ/Messiah and the Son of God. For us as readers there is no "messianic secret." The empty tomb account in 16:1–8 leaves us wondering whether Jesus did appear to his disciples in Galilee and whether the women did get out the message about Jesus' resurrection from the dead. The final episode, and indeed all the ironies in Mark, leave "the reader with a deep sense that more is going on than meets the eye, that this story—including its catastrophe—is meaningful in a dimension not readily available on the surface" (p. 177).

Space and Time

In *Narrative Space and Mythic Meaning in Mark* (1988), **Elizabeth Struthers Malbon** develops her study around three interrelated centers of interest: the meaning of Mark's Gospel, the significance of space in a narrative, and the exegetical potential of structural analysis. Her work is an adaptation of the methodology of the French structural anthropologist Claude Lévi-Strauss for analyzing myth. She seeks to consider all Markan spatial locations in their system of relationships and the significance of this manifest narrative system in terms of the underlying, nonmanifest, "mythological" system.

In investigating Markan spatial order, Malbon treats three major kinds of space: geopolitical space (named regions, cities, and towns, such as Galilee and Jerusalem), topographical space (physical features, such as the sea, the wilderness, mountains), and architectural space (human-made structures, such as houses, synagogues, and the temple). She deals with each suborder of spatial relations in three steps: isolating the relations, examining the sequence, and analyzing the schema.

The goal of Malbon's structural analysis is not so much locating, for example, the "wilderness" in terms of first-century Palestinian geography, but rather understanding the significance of the "wilderness" in terms of Markan spatial relations in which it is embedded and in terms of the larger traditional system of associations of the "wilderness" presupposed by Mark.

With regard to geopolitical space, Mark's narrative begins in Judea with John the Baptist's activity (1:5), concentrates on Galilee (1:14—9:50), moves to Jerusalem (10:1—16:8), and points forward to appearances of the risen Jesus in Galilee (see 14:28 and 16:7). In topographical space, the "way" (or road) represents the final mediation of this suborder that encompasses heaven versus earth, land versus sea, and isolated areas versus inhabited areas. In architectural space, the chief oppositions are house versus synagogue and temple, room versus courtyard, and tomb versus temple, with an underlying opposition between profane and sacred. Ironically the architectural spaces most closely related with Jesus (house, room, tomb) belong to the profane pole of the oppositions. In the final analysis, however, Mark's story of Jesus bears witness to "the breakdown of the opposition of the sacred and the profane and the breakthrough to a new reality" (p. 140).

When Malbon comes to integrate the geopolitical, topographical, and architectural dimensions of narrative space in Mark's Gospel, she gives special attention to the "way" as the final mediator between the various oppositions. The "way" for Mark signals not so much another place as it does a road between places, a dynamic process of movement. Indeed, Jesus being "on the way" as suggested by Mark 16:7 ("he is going ahead of you to Galilee") is the key mediator of all the various Markan manifestations of the fundamental opposition of order versus chaos.

Malbon notes that the Markan Jesus has an affinity for "the space between"—the way (between isolated areas and inhabited areas), the mountain (between heaven and earth), the Sea of Galilee (between the Jewish homeland and foreign lands), and the tomb (between outside and inside). Thus Mark's Gospel closes with the spatial image of Jesus being "on the way" to Galilee (16:7), suggesting that the conflict between the chaos and the order of life is overcome not in arriving but in being on the way.

According to Mark's narrative the first words that Jesus utters concern time: "The time *[kairos]* is fulfilled" (1:15). In *Crisis and Continuity: Time in the Gospel of Mark* (1998), **Brenda Deen Schildgen** takes a literary and hermeneutical-philosophical approach to exploring the various aspects of time. She considers how Mark's "crisis time narrative connects ordinary or real living local time with 'universal' or mythic time because the narrative has both a historical reality and a symbolic reality that undergird the mythic time of the Gospel and make claims for all-time eternal truth" (p. 18). Her investigation concerns five dimensions of time in Mark: present, past, suspended, mythic, and ritual.

In his first-century context (his present), Mark used elements from various popular and contemporary literary forms: Hebraic history, fiction, apocalypses, and biography. He did so in order to present Jesus as a wonder-working, wandering teacher, who violates contemporary social, religious, and political habits and behavior, until his death when order is restored. In his narrative world of ordinary time, Mark subjects the present to critical scrutiny (as in a picaresque novella).

The past dimension in Mark's concept of time is supplied chiefly by Old Testament quotations and allusions. With them Mark establishes continuity with the textual tradition of "Israel," and shows that the laws as well as the historical and emotional experiences recorded in that textual tradition still have relevance to the present as commentary, contrast, or hopes both denied or still possible. Schildgen observes: "There is little triumphalism in the gathering of the scattered words of the past; rather it is hoped that this past will be remembered, retrieved, and continued in the present" (p. 93).

Suspended time is a feature in one of Mark's most famous literary devices — intercalation or the "sandwich" in which one narrative is interrupted by another, and then the first is rejoined and completed. The effect on the reader is to suspend time or at least its linear dimensions, and to construct relationships among the parts. The sandwiched parts generally feature "marginal" characters, and while halting the main story line, they develop many of the central themes of the Gospel.

Mythic time is a critical moment when overcoming the fragmented human condition is presented as a possibility. Mark presents Jesus' public ministry as a liminal interruption of "normal" time in which Jesus accepts both the promise and the vulnerability of his mission and his role in it. The way of Jesus is portrayed as a human possibility and a utopian hope for the present and the future.

Ritual time in Mark is best represented in the two feeding miracles (6:30–44, 8:1–10), and by way of contrast, in Herod's banquet (6:14–29). Schildgen describes ritual time in Mark as a "subversive flicker," a gap between ordinary time and the return to ordinary time. She also uses the expression "the green world" to refer to a second or alternate world to the normal world. The Last Supper (14:12–25) is more complicated and paradoxical than the feeding miracles. According to Schildgen, in the Last Supper all the temporal conditions are played out: "history versus eternity; the present against the future; the historical against the 'mythic'" (p. 155). Thus the Last Supper enacts the "aporia of time"—the indeterminate end of ritual time.

Characters

According to **Jack Dean Kingsbury** in *Conflict in Mark: Jesus, Authorities, Disciples* (1989), the force that drives forward Mark's Gospel is the element of conflict. At the core of the conflict is Jesus as the central character. His struggle is, on the one hand, with Israel (the religious authorities and the crowd) and, on the other hand, with the disciples.

Mark's story takes place in "the time of fulfillment" (between "the time of prophecy" and the full establishment of God's rule in power) and in the land of Israel. The major characters are Jesus the protagonist, the religious authorities who serve as the antagonists, the disciples who are at once loyal to Jesus and uncomprehending of him, the crowd that is at once well-disposed toward Jesus and without faith in him, and those groups of minor characters who either exhibit faith or somehow exemplify what it means to serve. Kingsbury divides Mark's plot into a beginning (1:1–13), a middle (1:14—8:26), and an end (8:27—16:8). In the three chapters of his literary analysis, Kingsbury traces the theme of conflict in Mark through these three phases with reference to the stories of Jesus, the religious authorities, and the disciples, respectively.

The beginning (1:1–13) provides the reader with essential information about Jesus' true identity as the Son of God, while the middle (1:14—8:26) shows him to be a wise teacher (even a prophet) and a powerful healer who nonetheless finds little or no comprehension among his own people. The end (8:27—16:8) leads the reader through the process of coming to recognize Jesus in turn as the Messiah, the Son of David, and the Son of God. Only at the moment of Jesus' death on the cross does a human character (in this case the centurion) grasp that Jesus really is the Son of God (15:39). Thus, through Jesus' death and resurrection, Mark's story reaches its climax and comes to a fundamental resolution. The final resolution will take place with Jesus' return at the end of this age (see Mark 13).

The "authorities" form a united front in the relentless opposition that they mount against Jesus. They include the Pharisees, Sadducees, Herodians, chief priests, scribes, and elders. In their role as the antagonists of Jesus they can be treated as a single character. Their story reveals how little real authority they have, whereas Jesus proves to be Israel's true shepherd and royal Son of God. As Jesus' conflict with the religious authorities unfolds in the middle section (1:14—8:26), it becomes progressively more intense in both tone and content. In the end section (8:27—16:8), Jesus' conflict with the religious authorities takes place principally in the temple and eventually involves the Roman political authority (Pontius Pilate) in putting Jesus to death. The result is that Jesus supersedes the temple as the "place" of salvation and becomes the founder and ruler of God's end-time people.

In the first half of the middle of Mark's Gospel (1:14—8:26), the disciples chosen by Jesus give him their undivided loyalty while being with Jesus and sharing in his mission. In the latter half, however, they show themselves to be increasingly uncomprehending. In the end (8:27—16:8), the conflict between Jesus and his disciples becomes critical—to the point where the disciples abandon Jesus during the passion narrative. Nevertheless, Jesus' promise that the disciples will see him again in his risen state (14:27; see also 16:7) suggests that their conflict will be resolved. Kingsbury describes how Mark leaves the disciples at the end of his Gospel in this way: "Reconciled to Jesus and viewing reality from his standpoint, the disciples move toward the future as Jesus described this for them in his eschatological discourse of chapter 13" (p. 117).

In *Other Followers of Jesus: Minor Characters as Major Figures in Mark's Gospel* (1994), **Joel F. Williams** explores the role of some "minor" figures who step forth from the crowd in affecting the reader's response to Mark's story of Jesus. His thesis is that "Mark's narrative includes certain minor characters who live up to the demands and ideals of Jesus, and thus who serve to instruct the reader further in the proper response to Jesus" (p. 206).

The episode about Bartimaeus (10:46–52) has a pivotal role in Mark's narrative, according to Williams. Before that passage Mark interweaves minor characters into his portrait of Jesus and the disciples in various ways. In 1:1 — 3:35, minor characters such as the possessed man, Peter's mother-in-law, the leper, and so forth, are needy persons who evoke sympathy and compassion from Jesus (and from the reader). In 4:1 — 8:21, figures such as the Gerasene demoniac, Jarius, the woman with the flow of blood, and so on, show great courage and faith in contrast to Jesus' own disciples. But in 8:22 — 10:45, the blind man of Bethsaida, the man with the possessed boy, and the rich man exhibit a kind of ambivalence that moves the reader to focus even more on the paradigmatic nature of Jesus and his message.

In Mark 10:46–52 Bartimaeus appears as both an exemplary follower and a transitional figure. He cries out for mercy, and his repeated cries show that he is trusting, persistent, and courageous. Bartimaeus is believing and sincere, and so Jesus heals him of his blindness. At the end of the story he is healed, sighted, and saved. As both supplant and exemplar he is a transitional figure in the narrative, and stands at the beginning of a series of minor characters who function in the narrative as exemplary figures. Thus the reader is encouraged to move beyond faith in Jesus to a more faithful following of Jesus.

Following the Bartimaeus story, various minor characters emerge from the crowd and respond to Jesus in remarkably positive ways. They include the scribe, the poor widow, the woman who anoints Jesus, Simon of Cyrene, the centurion, the women at the cross, and Joseph of Arimathea. The reader is encouraged to identify with these figures.

However, the women who go to the tomb on Easter morning are portrayed somewhat ambiguously. After moving the reader to identify with them positively, Mark creates a distance from them due to their apparent disobedience: "and they said nothing to anyone, for they were afraid" (16:8b). According to Williams, the reader is being led to acknowledge that failure, fear, and disobedience are still possible in the period between the resurrection and the Parousia.

That Jesus is the central character in Mark's Gospel is clear, while his disciples and opponents serve to instruct readers on the demands of following Jesus and the difficulties that it may involve. In a collection of essays entitled *In the Company of Jesus: Characters in Mark's Gospel* (2000), **Elizabeth Struthers Malbon** contends that basic to the working of Mark's story is the interaction and interrelation of its characters. She notes that many of the women (and men) followers of Jesus are portrayed as fallible. There are bold women and faithful women (5:24–34, 7:24–30), self-denying women and serving women (12:41–44, 14:3–9), women followers from beginning to end (15:40–41, 15:47 — 16:8). The message is that anyone can be a follower but no one finds it easy. Likewise, Jesus' disciples and the crowds are presented with both strong and weak points to serve as realistic and encouraging models for hearers/readers who experience both strength and weakness in their Christian discipleship. In other essays on the disciples, the Jewish leaders, and the poor widow of 12:41–44, respectively, Malbon explores how the context influences the presentation of the characters and our perceptions of them.

Genre

What is Mark's Gospel? What kind of book is it? In *Sowing the Gospel: Mark's World in Literary-Historical Perspective* (1989), **Mary Ann Tolbert** addresses what she perceives as two basic problems in Markan research: the absence of a consistent interpretation of the Gospel in all its parts, and the apparently obscure and even muddled character of Mark's narrative.

In her literary-historical analysis, Tolbert contends that these problems can be solved in large part by situating Mark's Gospel within the literary currents of its own historical milieu. She argues that this Gospel is best understood as belonging to the realm of popular culture and popular literature in the Greco-Roman world.

In particular, according to Tolbert, Mark's Gospel belongs by way of its literary genre with the ancient Greek novels: Chariton's *Chaereas and Callirhoe,* Xenophon's *An Ephesian Tale,* Longus's *Daphnis and Chloe,* Achilles Tatius's *Leucippe and Clitophon,* and Heliodorus's *An Ethiopian Tale.* Most of these are "erotic" novels in the sense that their plots involve the god Eros. Having identified Mark with this genre, Tolbert quickly denies that it is an ancient novel of the erotic type. Rather, her point is that its mix of historiographic form and dramatic force, its synthesis of earlier genres (such as biography, memorabilia of a sage, aretalogy, and apocalypse), its stylistic techniques of episodic plot beginning with minimal introduction and moving to central turning point and final recognition scene, and most of all, its fairly crude, repetitious, and conventionalized narrative—all these display striking *stylistic* similarities to the popular Greek ancient novel.

Her contention is that to its original or authorial audience, Mark's Gospel was readily understood as popular literature; that is, literature composed in such a way as to be accessible to a wide spectrum of society. The problem is that popular literature from one culture is especially difficult for readers from another culture.

And this is the reason why Mark can seem opaque and muddled to modern readers.

The bulk of Tolbert's work is a literary analysis of the entire Gospel of Mark, and it contains many fresh and even brilliant literary insights. Taking as her starting point the parable of the sower and its interpretation in 4:1–20, she regards the first major part of Mark (1:14 – 10:52) as concerned primarily with Jesus' mission of sowing the word and the responses of the various types of ground, and the second major part (11:1 – 16:8) as dominated by the issue of Jesus' identity and the inevitable results that its publication or revelation draws. In this outline the parables of the sower (4:3–9) and of the vineyard (11:1–11) are pivotal. While referring often to the rhetorical conventions of the ancient Greek novels, many of her most astute literary observations can stand on their own.

Then Tolbert moves from literary analysis to draw historical and theological conclusions. She concludes that, when read in its proper ancient literary milieu, Mark's Gospel is neither opaque nor muddled but rather fairly simple. She is skeptical about attempts to tie the Gospel's composition to a specific crisis in a specific community, though she inclines toward the traditional Roman origin and imagines that the Gospel was read aloud and intended for a wide audience. She concludes that the Gospel of Mark was not written in response to the problems of a specific, local community but was intended, as were the ancient erotic novels, for a wide readership. She also maintains that it was written to individuals, not to groups, and individuals in primarily two general categories: individual Christians experiencing persecutions because of their faith, who were in need of encouragement, and individuals interested in Christianity but not yet fully committed, who needed to be persuaded. Thus Mark's rhetorical goals were both exhortation and proselytism.

Tolbert is also skeptical about using Mark's Gospel as a source for what really happened or for reliable information about the historical Jesus. Rather, she assumes that Mark's Gospel is primarily "fiction," analyzes it as fiction, and concludes that it is fiction. Moreover, she regards as especially inadequate Mark's theology "that only direct divine intervention can preserve the elect from the mess this generation is making of the cosmos" (p. 310). Instead, she proposes that Christians today work with others to bring God's kingdom to fruition.

Christopher Bryan's *A Preface to Mark: Notes on the Gospel in Its Literary and Cultural Settings* (1993) is a learned and eloquent exploration of two basic questions concerning the literary character of Mark's Gospel: What kind of text is Mark? and Was Mark written to be read aloud? The answers to these questions will naturally determine much about what we can and cannot expect from Mark's Gospel.

Bryan's first question concerns the literary genre or type of Mark's Gospel. In answering this question Bryan proposes to work chiefly with texts roughly parallel in time (ca. 100 BCE to 175 CE) and in sociocultural setting (Greco-Roman and Jewish). Rejecting the idea that the Gospels are totally *sui generis,* he proposes that they have most in common with the Greco-Roman "biography" or *bios.*

To prove his thesis, Bryan identifies themes and motifs that are generic to the Hellenistic "lives" and shows that most of these occur also in Mark's Gospel. Bryan's "cluster" of generic features in developing the case for taking Mark as a *bios* includes the opening statement or prologue that plunges us into the story (Mark 1:1–8), the sharp focus on the person of Jesus the sage as the main subject, the geographical setting of his story (Galilee, the way, Jerusalem), the chronological arrangement (with some references backward and forward), Jesus as a real and surprising character, the use of common motifs (the deeds and the death of the hero), the language of popular written style, the possibility of reading the whole text aloud (in about two hours) and of its being understood by everyone present, and the fulfillment of the functions of entertainment and edification.

From this cluster of themes and motifs found both in the Greco-Roman biographies and in Mark's Gospel, Bryan concludes that "granted its unusual features, it is as an example of a 'life' that Mark's text would have been received by an averagely educated Greco-Roman audience" (p. 62).

Bryan's second question— Was Mark written to be read aloud?—concerns how Mark's Gospel would have been communicated in the first century. Its written form, of course, is what has come down to us as part of the New Testament canon. But the milieu in which it was first "written" was largely an oral culture, and it was common practice then that written works be read aloud in a communal setting. On this matter Bryan's thesis is that "Mark was designed for oral transmission—and for transmission as a continuous whole—rather than for private study or silent reading" (p. 152).

His answer to the second question is established also by a "cluster" approach. Bryan first assembles a list of characteristics that are typical of and point to oral composition. He is not saying that Mark was a purely oral composition. Rather, he contends that the Gospel was produced with oral presentation in mind as the primary mode of its circulation, and that it reflects the use of the techniques of oral composition.

Those techniques include the uses of memorable incidents in story form (*chreiai* or narratives that lead up to a memorable teaching, miracle stories, the hero's death), hyperbole or exaggeration, parataxis ("and...and" units), memorable formulas, concentric and chiastic structures, and an overall outline that would facilitate comprehension by attentive listeners. All these features are prominent in Mark's Gospel. Even when Mark uses the Jewish Scriptures as part of his presentation, it is generally by way of allusion or adaptation, rather than by exact quotation of any known written version.

Given the setting of the Gospel's composition in the Greco-Roman world of the first century, Bryan reasons that the Evangelist must have been educated in a system that assumed that writers wrote their works to be read aloud. He even paints a portrait of Mark "the note taker" as a Greek-speaking Christian of (probably)

Jewish descent absorbing what he heard and writing down the traditions associated with Jesus in a simple and popular style to produce a work that might be read aloud for interest and edification. This picture is not far from what Papias (in Eusebius, *Ecclesiastical History* 3.39.15) and other patristic writers say about the Evangelist known as Mark.

Conclusion

These literary studies of Mark illustrate how old and new literary methods can be combined to show how this Gospel "works" as a book, and what effects it might have on attentive readers in antiquity and today. From these studies, Mark emerges as a very competent author. While their main focus is the text of Mark's Gospel, it does not take much effort to perceive that these various literary approaches can contribute to a better theological appreciation of the Gospel's significance and can raise historical questions about its composition, background, and genre.

The dangers encountered in employing these literary approaches include getting lost in literary theory and forcing the text into frameworks foreign to it, producing readings that are too subtle or precious (especially if the Gospel was first communicated mainly in oral performances), and dislodging the text from any historical reality. Many of the literary approaches applied to Mark's Gospel in recent years were developed for analyzing novels and other works of fiction. But to regard Mark's Gospel as simply a historical novel does not seem appropriate to its author's intention (or what can be known about it) and the long history of its interpretation.

3
Theological Studies

Whatever merits Mark's Gospel may have as a work of literature, it is first and foremost a religious text. It describes the teaching and healing ministry of Jesus of Nazareth, makes exalted claims about his person (Messiah, Son of God, Son of Man, etc.), and tells the story of his passion and death. Moreover, by occasional direct quotations and by many allusions, Mark's Gospel seeks to establish this Jesus as the fulfillment of the Scriptures of Israel. From the very start of the Gospel, Jesus calls for a response: "Repent, and believe in the good news....Follow me...." (1:15, 17). Some respond immediately to his call but later waver. Others reject it totally, treat Jesus with hostility, and even put him to death.

An Overview of Markan Theology

William R. Telford in *The Theology of the Gospel of Mark* (1999) seeks to provide a comprehensive presentation of Mark's religious understanding, ideas, and beliefs about God, Jesus, the human condition, the world, and the end of the world. He develops his profile of Mark's theology in dialogue with the text of Mark's Gospel, several generations of Markan scholars, and the other books of the New Testament. In reaching and defending his own views, Telford provides a bridge between the older material covered by Frank Matera and what is treated in this sequel. Telford contends that Mark's basic purpose was christological and soteriological. That is, Mark was concerned about correcting a false Christology prevalent in the church, and about teaching both a true Christology and its consequences for Christian theology. The Christology that Mark combated, according to Telford, went back to the Jerusalem church and viewed Jesus as only the victorious royal Messiah, the Son of David. The Christology that Mark promoted regarded Jesus as the divine but unrecognized Son of God whose suffering and death on the cross were redemptive. In Mark's christological-soteriological outlook there was an increasing emphasis on realized eschatology: "Jesus 'the Proclaimer' of the coming eschatological Kingdom of God is in the process of being seen as 'the Proclaimed' in whose person and ministry the Kingdom was (in another sense) *already* present" (p. 86).

Likewise, the miracle stories were integrated into Mark's epiphany Christology to portray him as a "divine man" having a supernatural status. And the fact of Jesus' death brought about the transformation of the glorious Son of Man into a suffering figure. The blindness of Jesus' opponents and of his own disciples also served to enhance Mark's "secret" Christology by providing many examples of Jesus being misunderstood and rejected.

Telford regards Mark as a Gentile Gospel that attacked the primitive Jewish-Christian community for both its resistance to Jesus' status as the Son of God and its resistance to the Gentile mission. He views Mark's soteriological emphasis—the salvific death of Jesus and the universality of salvation engendered by it—as bringing Mark and Paul into the same theological orbit.

While primarily concerned with describing Mark's religious ideas in their first-century context, Telford also reflects on Mark's enduring theological significance. He regards the Gospel's combination of Christology and discipleship as posing a special challenge for people today, its emphasis on spirituality and interiority as being salutary, and its theology of the cross as raising questions about the ideology of power. However, Telford is not convinced that Mark is especially positive in his portrayals of women ("they are no better than their male counterparts," p. 234). And he observes that Mark's Gospel is a good candidate to be described as "anti-Semitic" in its depictions of various Jewish characters and in its Christian theological claims vis-à-vis Judaism.

In my opinion, Telford's synthetic study of the theology of Mark's Gospel is disappointing. The author has edited an excellent collection of classic essays on Mark entitled *The Interpretation of Mark* (2nd ed., 1995) and is thoroughly conversant with the history of Markan scholarship. But his own synthetic work seems too concerned with rescuing dubious scholarly hypotheses and approaches (such as the "divine man" Christology, corrective Christology, and the messianic secret) that are better left in the past. The book is more in tune with the scholarship of the previous generation than with that of the period covered in this book.

Christology

One of the most striking features of Mark's Gospel is the abundance of miracle stories. The twenty-one units that can be identified as miracle stories fall into five thematic categories: exorcisms, healings, epiphanies, curses, and combinations. In *Teaching with Authority: Miracles and Christology in the Gospel of Mark* (1992), **Edwin K. Broadhead** uses narrative analysis of the Markan miracle stories to investigate what and how they contribute to Mark's portrait of Jesus.

After explaining what narrative analysis is and why it is an appropriate tool for studying the Markan miracle accounts and Markan Christology, Broadhead examines each of the twenty-one miracle narratives with regard to its narrative morphology (the motifs or elements that make up the text) and its narrative syntax (how the motifs are arranged, interact, and communicate). He also considers how each miracle story fits within the larger unit of the Gospel and how the unit as a whole contributes to the Gospel's overall portrait of Jesus.

For example, in treating the stilling of the storm (Mark 4:35–41), Broadhead first plots out the various elements in the narrative (morphology), explores the dynamism that governs them (syntax), and considers the passage's relationship with the surrounding material. He divides Mark's Gospel into six large units (1:1—3:7a, 3:7b—6:6a, 6:6b—8:27a, 8:27b—10:52, 11:1—13:37, and 14:1—16:8) and shows how the miracle stories in each unit add to the development of the Christology of the entire Gospel. So he concludes that "through the formal strategy of the narrative the miracle stories of Mark 3:7—6:6 now characterize Jesus as wondrous and mighty teacher, suffering servant, caller of disciples" (p. 116).

From the narrative analysis of the individual miracle stories Broadhead draws some more general conclusions. He rejects the idea that the Markan miracle stories reflect a "divine man" *(theios anēr)* Christology, as well as the notion that Mark's Gospel represents a corrective to an overemphasis on Jesus' miracles among some early Christians. Instead, he contends that Mark's Gospel offers a unified narrative portrait of Jesus as "the powerful proclaimer whose wondrous teachings lead to his death" (p. 213). He finds no christological dichotomy between the Jesus of the miracles and the Jesus of the cross.

Broadhead summarizes the Christology of the Markan miracle stories in the following way: "The miracle stories portray Jesus as the mighty preacher/teacher, the powerful healer, the exorcist without equal, the priestly servant of God. Jesus is the caller of disciples, the creator of community, the ruler over chaos, the epiphany of God's power and presence, God's compassionate shepherd. Jesus is the prophet of old who founds the new community of faith. Jesus is the giver of life who journeys to his death in Jerusalem. Jesus is the revered son of David and the beloved Son of God" (p. 216).

Broadhead continued his study of Markan Christology through narrative analysis in *Prophet, Son, Messiah: Narrative Form and Function in Mark 14–16* (1994). For each pericope in the Markan passion narrative he provides an examination of its narrative morphology and narrative syntax, as well as a comparative analysis. For example, when treating the anointing scene in Mark 14:1–11, Broadhead first lists the five major motifs: the leaders conspire; the woman anoints; some complain; Jesus responds; and the leaders conspire. Then he shows how these elements work together to link Jesus' mission as teacher and prophet with his destiny in the passion. Finally by looking at the parallel texts (Matt 26:1–16; Luke 7:36–50; John 12:1–8), he highlights Mark's strategy in placing the anointing story at the juncture of Jesus' public ministry and his passion.

From the series of narrative analyses there emerges a better sense of the complex and profound characterization of Jesus in the Markan passion narrative: "He is the true prophet and messiah, the Son of God. He is the suffering Son of Man who will come in power and glory. He is innocent and righteous, the Suffering Servant, the Crucified One" (pp. 270–71). These various christological images all cluster around the event of the crucifixion. And Broadhead uses his literary methods with particular effectiveness in examining the literary and theological dimensions of the scene of Jesus' death on the cross in Mark 15:20c–37: "Jesus is the rejected prophet, the slain Son, the crucified messiah" (p. 211).

Taking as his starting point the narrative analysis of the Markan passion account, Broadhead stresses the coherence and unity of the characterization of Jesus within Mark 14–16. Moreover, he finds a reciprocal relationship in Christology between the stories of Jesus' public ministry in chapters 1–13 and the scenes in Mark 14–16. This reciprocity in turn leads Broadhead to argue against the theories that the Markan passion narrative represents corrective Christology (the cross) to the miracle-worker Christology of chapters 1–13, or that the passion account was the earliest part of the Gospel tradition that then attracted other disparate materials associated with Jesus. Rather, according to Broadhead, "[f]rom beginning to end Jesus is the wondrous teacher and prophet, Son of God, Son of Man, the suffering messiah" (p. 282). From his narrative analysis Broadhead proposes the following definition of the Gospel genre: "[A] Gospel is a narrative account of Jesus' messianic life, death and resurrection shaped by and for the task of proclamation" (p. 286).

In yet another book on Markan Christology, *Naming Jesus: Titular Christology in the Gospel of Mark* (1999), **Broadhead** analyzes the literary patterns and strategies employed in the naming of Jesus. He treats the following titles: Jesus the Nazarene, prophet, the greater one, priest, king, teacher, shepherd, the Holy One of God, the Suffering Servant of God, Son of David, Son of God, Son of Man, Lord, Christ, the risen one, and the crucified one. He concludes that Mark shaped and reshaped numerous images of Jesus into a stream of titular Christology, and describes Mark's naming of Jesus as a "christening" and a "christologizing."

Use of the Old Testament

While there are relatively few explicit Old Testament quotations in Mark's Gospel, the entire narrative is shot through with biblical allusions, and the major events are pegged upon them. The most far-ranging treatment of Mark's use of the Old Testament is **Joel Marcus's** *The Way of the Lord: Christological Exegesis of the Old Testament in the Gospel of Mark* (1992). He contends that Mark retained a commitment to the "old, old story" of the Jewish Scriptures while reading them through the lens of Jesus' life, death, and resurrection.

Marcus treats Mark's christological exegesis of the Old Testament according to the following outline: the gospel according to Isaiah (Mark 1:2–3); the beloved, well-pleasing Son (1:9–11); the transfigured Son of God (9:2–8); the suffering Son of Man and his forerunner (9:11–13); the rejected and vindicated stone

(12:10–11); David's Son and David's Lord (12:35–37); and the passion narrative (14–16), as presented in the light of Zechariah 9–14, Daniel 7, the Psalms of the Righteous Sufferer (especially Psalm 22), and the Deutero-Isaian Servant Songs. In analyzing Mark's use of the Old Testament, Marcus develops and is guided by four methodological principles. The first principle is to look to the larger context in which the text appears. For example, of the several texts quoted in 1:2–3 (Exod 23:20; Mal 3:1; Isa 40:3), Mark's attribution of all of them simply to "Isaiah" is intended, according to Marcus, as a clue to the reader to keep in mind all of Second Isaiah (chaps. 40–55) and its themes of the divine warrior, the wilderness, the way through the desert, and the arrival at Jerusalem. The problem here is knowing precisely how much of the larger context is being evoked.

The second principle is to be sensitive to Mark's use of Jewish exegetical methods and interpretive traditions. For example, in explaining Mark 9:11–13, Marcus shows how rabbinic literature deals with apparent contradictions or tensions between biblical texts. He shows how Mark reinterprets the base verse (Mal 3:22: Elijah will come before the Messiah) in terms of the contrastive verse (the scriptural expectation that the Son of Man will suffer and be rejected) and reconciles them in light of an implicit syllogism: Since Jesus is a suffering Messiah, his forerunner must be a suffering Elijah. Likewise, Marcus frequently points to Jewish traditions surrounding these texts in rabbinic writings, and calls attention to the eschatological framework that they are given. The problem here is the relatively late date (from 200 CE onward) of the rabbinic compilations.

The third methodological principle is to recognize that for Mark Christ is the key to understanding the Old Testament Scriptures. Marcus notes that in Mark "the entire Old Testament is read through the lens of the crucified Messiah." But he also observes that the movement of thought "is not exclusively from Christ to the scripture but also from scripture christologically construed to a deeper understanding of the events surrounding Christ" (p. 108).

Each chapter in the book illustrates the interaction between the person of Jesus and the Old Testament Scriptures. The problem is whether and how it is possible to separate "historical" data from biblical interpretation, and how one can be sure what is "history" and what is "midrash."

The fourth principle is to be aware how Mark uses scripture to address the needs of the community for which and in which he wrote his Gospel. Marcus repeatedly refers to his article "The Jewish War and the *Sitz im Leben* of Mark" in *Journal of Biblical Literature* (1992) in which he claims that Mark's Gospel reflects the pervasive influence on his community of the First Jewish Revolt (66–74 CE), an event to which the Markan community stood in both geographical and temporal proximity.

What emerges from Marcus's analysis of Mark's christological exegesis of the Old Testament in *The Way of the Lord* is a "high" Son of God Christology (with hints at Jesus' divinity) related to the kingdom of God and placed in the framework of "the way of the Lord" portrayed in Isaiah 40–55. And over everything is the mystery of the cross. Marcus observes that "there seems to be no Jewish parallel for Mark's thought that the Messiah's kingship and the kingdom of God are manifest already and in a definitive way in his suffering and death" (p. 202).

Two published doctoral dissertations have affirmed the importance of the book of Isaiah for Mark and the value of looking to the larger contexts of his Old Testament quotations and allusions. In *Isaiah in the Gospel of Mark I–VIII* (1994), **Richard Schneck** contends that there is at least one significant reference to the book of Isaiah in each of the first eight chapters of Mark, and that the book of Isaiah was quite influential in shaping the plot and Christology of the Gospel. He agrees with Marcus that by his biblical quotations and allusions Mark conjures up the larger context of the Old Testament passage. While showing that the Evangelist had a definite predilection for Isaiah over other biblical books, Schneck also suggests that Isaiah references were embedded in the early stages of the Jesus tradition, and that the process of adapting Isaiah and the other scriptures may well go back to Jesus himself.

Likewise **Rikki E. Watts** in *Isaiah's New Exodus and Mark* (1997; 2000) argues that Mark's fundamental hermeneutics for interpreting and presenting Jesus derives from Isaiah's new-exodus motif and Malachi's warning, which are quoted together in Mark 1:2–3. Watts views these texts as evoking their full Old Testament contexts and as providing the programs for Mark's entire narrative about Jesus. He concludes that Mark's primary concern was to present Jesus as the one who unexpectedly fulfills the hope of Isaiah's long delayed "new exodus."

Discipleship

One of the persistent puzzles in modern Markan scholarship has been the mixed (and often negative) portrayal of Jesus' first disciples. On the one hand, they get off to a remarkably positive start. They respond immediately and generously to Jesus' call ("Follow me!"), leaving behind their former ways of life to be with Jesus and to share in his mission of proclaiming God's kingdom by teaching and healing. On the other hand, beginning in Mark 4, these same disciples become increasingly obtuse with regard to the person and values of Jesus. In the passion narrative (Mark 14–15), they all fall away, most egregiously in the cases of Judas, who hands Jesus over to be killed, and Peter, who denies Jesus three times.

In *Our Journey with Jesus: Discipleship according to Mark* (1987), **Dennis M. Sweetland** presents an analysis of texts in Mark's Gospel that pertain to the theme of discipleship and uses this theme as a means of understanding Mark's theological significance as a whole. While offering mainly a description of the Markan textual evidence, there is also a contemporary theological purpose at work: "The appropriate response of individuals today is the same as it was when Mark wrote his Gospel" (p. 163).

Intended for a general audience, Sweetland's study of discipleship according to Mark remains an accurate and accessible synthesis of other scholars' research and a balanced and comprehensive reading of the pertinent passages. By exploring one of the great Markan themes, he also provides access to the Evangelist's overall theological vision and shows how that vision might shape and challenge the lives of Christians today. It is a good example of biblical theology based on one book.

Sweetland takes as his starting point the various "call stories" in Mark, not only those that pertain directly to Jesus' disciples (1:16–20, 2:13–17, 3:13–19, 6:7–13) but also the (failed) call of the rich man (10:17–22). In these accounts Jesus takes the initiative and calls others to be with him and to continue his ministry of preaching, teaching, and healing. The Markan teachings about discipleship are found in passages dealing with the "disciples," the Twelve, others who "follow" Jesus, and even those who do not. They appear with special prominence in the Gospel's central section (8:22 — 10:52) where Jesus' disciples are forced to confront the mystery of the cross and the paradox that greatness in Jesus' community consists in serving others. Throughout the Gospel Jesus' disciples are portrayed as complex characters who display great generosity and amazing obtuseness. At times they provide readers "with an object lesson in how *not* to understand discipleship and Jesus" (p. 83). Nevertheless, their failures need not imply permanent or absolute misunderstanding (see 14:28 and 16:7).

Discipleship according to Mark is not a solitary adventure. Rather, disciples live both in a vertical relationship with God and Jesus and in a horizontal relationship with other disciples. Formed from those who seek to discern and to do God's will (3:31–35), the community of disciples constitutes the new family of Jesus (10:29–31) and live in watchful anticipation of the fullness of God's kingdom (13:33–37). This new community is open to all kinds of persons precisely because Mark's Jesus is "a unifier who breaks through ethnic and sexual barriers to present the good news to all" (p. 112). At the same time Mark takes care to place the disciple's religious practices (Eucharist, baptism, prayer) and involvement in social realities (marriage, children, possessions) in the framework of the mystery of the cross and Jesus' identity as God's Servant.

In order to find out who Jesus really is, the disciples (and Mark's readers) must follow him up to Jerusalem. There the true identity of Jesus becomes clear only at his "trial" before the Sanhedrin (14:61–62) and at the cross (15:21–39). While Messiah and Son of Man are prominent christological titles, the most important title is Son of God (see 1:1, 11; 9:7; 14:61; 15:39). But all these titles receive their deeper meaning from Jesus' identity as the Servant of the Lord (see Isa 52:13—53:12) and the Suffering Just One (Ps 22).

For Sweetland, the Markan theme of discipleship has symbolic significance not only for Jesus' first companions but also for disciples today. As he notes, Mark's Gospel challenges us to reassess our lifestyle and take the steps necessary to restructure our lives in accord with God's will and to follow the example of Jesus the Suffering Servant and Son of God (pp. 168–69).

How Jesus' first followers function rhetorically in Mark's Gospel is the subject of **Whitney Taylor Shiner's** 1992 Yale doctoral dissertation published as *Follow Me! Disciples in Markan Rhetoric* (1995). His study combines narrative criticism with comparative analysis. His thesis is that "the depiction of the disciples is subordinated thoroughly to what Mark wishes to say about Jesus at that particular point in his presentation" (p. 29).

For his comparative material Shiner chooses three Greek philosophical biographies—Xenophon's *Memorabilia* (about Socrates), Iamblichus's *Pythagorean Life,* and Philostratus's *Life of Apollonius of Tyana*—and one example of Jewish wisdom teaching, the *Wisdom of Ben Sira.* He explores how the Greek philosophical biographies use imperfect disciples to illustrate the lifestyle, thought, and teaching method of their philosophical heroes and to provide negative points of comparison for the exemplary character of their sages. What Ben Sira supplies is a partial explanation of why Jesus' disciples according to Mark seem so obtuse: Wisdom is ultimately a gift from God, and it takes time to receive, assimilate, and act upon this gift.

In the second part of his book, Shiner offers a rhetorical analysis of how the disciples function in Mark's Gospel, with reference to the four works chosen for comparison. He rejects theories about the Markan disciples as ciphers for specific (heretical) groups within the early church, and insists on the disciples' role in bringing out aspects of the person of Jesus (who himself is a kind of parable). Their incomprehension serves as the occasion for Jesus to provide good example and wise instruction. The disciples in their positive moments offer a sympathetic human perspective seriously engaged with Jesus and his significance. In their negative moments their incomprehension represents "the inability of the world to penetrate the mask of the mundane to comprehend the reality of Jesus" (p. 292). They illustrate for Mark's readers how hard it is to comprehend who Jesus really is.

Community Life

According to **Michael F. Trainor** in *The Quest for Home: The Household in Mark's Community* (2001), the household is the place for intimacy ("home") and becomes an overarching structure for reading and organizing Mark's Gospel. He develops this thesis first by investigating how people in the Greco-Roman world understood houses and households, and then by reading Mark's Gospel through the lens of the "household."

Trainor's work combines social-science analysis (describing the house/household as a social institution in antiquity) and literary criticism (following the motif of "house/household" through Mark's Gospel) in order to bring out a theme with theological significance. The social-science analysis of the ancient household draws upon the results of archaeology (excavations and reconstructions of ancient houses) and ancient philosophical texts (Plato, Aristotle, Cicero) to arrive at insights into what people in New Testament times experienced in their households and what they wished them to be. In his literary analysis or "reading," he traces the many references to "house" throughout Mark's Gospel and tries to discern where Mark takes for granted Greco-Roman social assumptions about the household and where he goes against them. What emerges on the theological level are intimations of a different way of structuring church life today—a model that is more open and local (the new family of Jesus) and less hierarchical and patriarchal (the Greco-Roman household/the Roman Catholic Church).

Trainor first offers a survey of the different kinds of houses in the Greco-Roman world. For understanding Mark's accounts about Jesus' ministry in Galilee, the most important types are the simple "four room" house and its expanded "courtyard" style version. For appreciating the context in which Mark's Gospel would have first been read and heard, the *domus* or "mansion" style house large enough to accommodate a local Christian community or "house church" would have to be imagined. Analysis of what ancient Greek writers (especially Plato and Aristotle) and Roman writers (Cicero) said about the household reveals the ideal of social harmony based on order and subordination, with special emphasis on the authority of the *paterfamilias*.

In this context Mark the Evangelist appears as both "pro-cultural" and "counter-cultural." On the one hand, Mark accepts the social significance of the household and makes it a key image in his narrative about Jesus. On the other hand, Mark rejects the authority of the *paterfamilias* and proposes a community/household in which God is the true father and there are no human "fathers" in the sense of figures with sole and ultimate authority. (Note the absence of "fathers" from the lists of members in the true family of Jesus in Mark 3:35 and 10:30.)

For his reading of Mark's Gospel from the "household" perspective, Trainor proposes the following general outline: the homeless wilderness (Mark 1:1–15), the gathering of the new household (1:16—3:35), strengthening the household (4:1—6:6), the missionary household (6:7—8:26), the suffering household (8:27—10:52), the household and the temple (11:1—13:37), and homelessness (14:1—16:8).

In this schema the "home" becomes the place of Jesus' healing, teaching, and ministering, and is an urban center in which the resurrection is tangibly experienced. While the household of Jesus is intended as a place of nurture for all its members, it nevertheless experiences problems and tensions—so much so that Trainor interprets the seven brutal questions raised by Jesus in Mark 8:17–21 ("Do you still not perceive or understand?") as directed not simply to the Twelve but rather to each generation of readers. In this situation Mark's household must purify its vision of Jesus and the place that suffering plays in his life while widening its doors to all kinds of marginal persons. The passion narrative brings both a heightened sense of homelessness as well as the assurance that in Christ's resurrection the final victory has been won and that God's presence may now be encountered more fully in the mysteries of everyday life.

Faith and Related Themes

In comparison with Luke's Gospel (which is sometimes called "the Gospel of prayer"), prayer is not a major topic in Mark's Gospel. The Markan Jesus does, however, teach about prayer (see 9:29, 11:17, 11:22–25, 12:40, 13:18, 14:38) and does model prayer in the Gethsemane episode (14:32–42) and in some other passages (see 1:35, 6:46, and 15:34). The most intriguing feature of the Markan prayer texts is the apparent tension between Mark 11:22–25, which encourages complete confidence in the prayer of petition ("it will be done for you"), and 14:32–42, in which Jesus' own petition ("remove this cup from me") is not answered.

In *Prayer, Power, and the Problem of Suffering: Mark 11:22–25 in the Context of Markan Theology* (1988), **Sharyn Echols Dowd** seeks to explain this apparent contradiction by a detailed analysis of the instruction on prayer and then by placing it in the wider framework of Mark's theology. She regards Mark the Evangelist not merely as a collector of traditions but as "a master of narrative theology" (p. 123); she considers the miracle stories to be a positive element in the Gospel's plan and disputes the "corrective Christology" thesis that was in vogue in the 1970s.

The prayer instruction in Mark 11:22–25 is, according to Dowd, closely tied to the cursing of the fig tree (11:12–14), the cleansing of the temple (11:15–19), and the withering of the fig tree (11:20–21). It functions as both a critical commentary on the Jerusalem temple cult ("you have made it a den of robbers") and a positive affirmation that the community gathered around Jesus is now the "house of prayer." The introductory exhortation in 11:22 ("Have faith in God") controls both the pair of sayings about faith as a condition for effective prayer (11:23–24) and the following saying about forgiveness as a condition for effective prayer (11:25).

Then in the light of parallels from Greco-Roman writings and from contemporary Jewish texts, Dowd explores the theological assumptions behind Mark 11:23–24. The God whom the Markan Jesus addresses as "Abba" is the God for whom all things are possible (14:36). God is the one who alone can move mountains. Dowd notes: "Affirmation of the omnipotence of God and of God's agency in the world is essential to Mark's theology of prayer" (pp. 93–94). In this context "faith" means to believe or hold to be true the worldview that asserts God's power to affect events in the world that are impossible for humans and for other natural agents to affect.

The assumption behind 11:25 is that mutual forgiveness within the community is the condition for the community's receiving forgiveness from God for its trespasses against God. The idea in this context is that God responds favorably to the prayers of the community that stands in right relationship with

God; that is, a community whose sins are forgiven. In the context of faith and mutual forgiveness, the community may pray for "anything," and "it will be done for them."

But how can this instruction about prayer be correlated with the apparent rejection of Jesus' petition ("remove this cup from me") in the Gethsemane pericope? Dowd explains the tension by arguing that in the Markan narrative Jesus' doing the will of God is manifested not only in his healing, preaching, and casting out of demons but also in his suffering and dying. She observes: "The [Gethsemane] scene is terrible, not because Jesus must suffer, but because his suffering is the will of the God who is powerful enough to prevent it, and who has eliminated so much in the narrative prior to this scene" (p. 158).

The point is that suffering, too, is part of God's will, and so Jesus (and his followers) must school himself to accept this reality. Thus Mark offers not a solution to the problem of theodicy but rather a way of coping with the tension that pervades Jesus' followers in their existence as empowered sufferers. Prayer in this setting functions as the practice in which the tension between power and suffering is faithfully maintained.

Mark employs the Greek words for "faith" *(pistis, pisteuein)* seventeen times in ten different episodes. In *Faith as a Theme of Mark's Narrative* (1989), **Christopher D. Marshall** investigates these passages and related texts from the perspective of narrative criticism, which he defines as the inquiry "into the relationship between the content of the story and the stylistic, compositional and rhetorical features of the narrative that convey the story to the reader" (p. 16).

The programmatic summary of Jesus' preaching in Mark 1:15 contains a call to "believe in the good news." Marshall takes this to mean "to respond in faith to the manifestation of God's kingdom as it is being brought about by the preaching of Jesus" (p. 47). The miracles of Jesus represent an implicit summons to repentance and faith for those who witness or hear them. They also illustrate the concrete benefits afforded to people of faith by the realization of the power of God's kingdom in Jesus. The recipients are powerless persons who nonetheless exhibit a stubborn faith in the presence of Jesus that leads to the operation of divine power on their behalf.

The theme of faith in Mark is related to becoming a disciple and remaining on "the way" of Jesus (see 1:16–20, 10:46–52). The instruction about faith, prayer, and forgiveness in 11:20–25 delineates the new community of faith that the disciples constitute. Indeed, Mark regards faith as the controlling and integrating factor in discipleship. The unbelief shown by the scribes and other opponents of Jesus is the refusal to accept his claims and demands out of fear of the consequences of doing so. The unbelief of Jesus' own disciples consists in their periodic failures to act in a manner that is consistent with their commitment to radical dependency on the power of Jesus.

According to Marshall, the object of faith in Mark's Gospel is Jesus inasmuch as he embodies the saving action of God. The context of faith is human need and helplessness. The necessity of faith is manifest in the perceptive dependence that is alone capable of receiving Jesus' deeds as revelatory acts of God. The experience of faith involves individuals in crisis situations, their knowledge or perception, and action (repentance, persistence, and obedience). The origin of faith is the realization of God's kingdom in Jesus' words and deeds that engenders faith in others. While the Markan Jesus functions chiefly as the object of faith, Mark may also picture Jesus as sharing the attitude of faith: "It is part of the paradox of the characterisation of Jesus that he is depicted both as the one who actualises God's presence and power, and one who exemplifies the response sought from others to this reality" (p. 240).

In *The Motif of Wonder in the Gospel of Mark* (1996), **Timothy Dwyer** argues that in Mark wonder is "a response to the divine intervention of the breaking-in of the kingdom or rule of God in power to save and restore the creation" (p. 198). Wonder may be a response to Jesus' teachings about God's kingdom and to his healing activities, as well as to Jesus' passion and resurrection, with all being viewed in light of the breaking-in of God's rule to save. The concentration of the "wonder" motif in 16:1–8 leaves the reader with a sense of dramatic awe.

In Mark's Gospel the reaction of "wonder" can take the form of astonishment, fear, terror, amazement, or awe. Of the thirty-two references to wonder in Mark, eight involve miracles or exorcisms (2:12; 4:41; 5:15, 33, 42; 6:50, 51; 7:37), eight occur in teaching or passion predictions (1:22, 27; 6:2; 9:32; 10:24, 26; 11:18; 12:17), three appear in the empty tomb narrative (16:5, 6, 8), five relate to the fear of Jewish or Gentile leaders (6:20; 11:32; 12:12; 15:5, 44), and eight are difficult to categorize (3:21; 5:20; 6:6; 9:6, 15; 10:32; 12:11; 14:33).

Dwyer first places the Markan motif of wonder in the context of Greco-Roman, early Jewish, and early Christian literature. Wonder in Greco-Roman literature appears mainly in reference to signs, portents, dreams, or divine intervention in general. In early Jewish writings wonder is a common reaction to God or God's actions, and appears frequently in eschatological, messianic, and/or propagandistic contexts. In early Christian texts, wonder may be a response to experiences that move one beyond that which is normal or natural into the realm of the supernatural. It can have either a positive or a negative connotation, and be followed by either faith or deception.

Then Dwyer provides exegetical analyses of each of the Markan "wonder" texts. In the first half of the Gospel, wonder follows the various acts of God in the breaking-in of God's kingdom in and through Jesus the Son of God. Many who experience those interventions of God through Jesus react with wonder, but not all proceed to repentance and faith. In the second half, the saving intervention of God takes the form of the Son of Man giving his life as a ransom for many (10:45), and this too elicits reactions of amazement.

What brings together all the references to wonder in Mark is the theme of the breaking-in of God's rule (1:14–15). God has acted by breaking in with divine rule to save, and the result is amazement. In the climax of the Gospel, the empty tomb narrative in 16:1–8, "wonder" appears three times (16:5, 6, 8). The fear shown by the women at the empty tomb yields to wonder at the mysterious ways of God, and their awed silence is only temporary. Viewed from the perspective of God's rule and the motif of "wonder," Mark's narrative is a story of the numinous and uncanny as well as of "good news." The good news is that the "Wholly Other," God, Yahweh, has come to rule and save through Jesus the Messiah. While humankind still trembles with wonder before the "Other," we are assured that God is good and is for us and with us in our human predicament.

Conclusion

The obituary for biblical theology has been written many times, but the discipline is alive and well. The term can be used to describe the detailed analysis of a specific biblical text to bring out its theological thought(s). Or it can refer to efforts at tracing a theme or motif through parts of the Bible or the entire Bible. When applied to the study of Mark's Gospel, biblical theology can take the form of a synthesis of all or many Markan themes (as in Telford's work). Or it can describe an examination of a particular theme or motif (perhaps in relation to other themes or motifs).

Most of the monographs covered in this chapter focus on particular topics or themes, and represent well what has been the way forward in recent Markan scholarship. Since they examine the relevant Markan texts in which their topic appears, all of these studies engage in literary criticism to a large extent. Most of these studies are "multidisciplinary" in that they do biblical theology in concert with other interpretive methods. Indeed, they illustrate the practical value of many of the "new" methods. For example, Broadhead makes effective use of narrative literary criticism in opening up various aspects of Markan Christology. In treating discipleship, Shiner does comparative analysis of the pertinent Markan texts with reference to three Greco-Roman texts and one Jewish text. And Trainor blends literary analysis, archaeology, the study of ancient parallels, and social-science perspectives in dealing with Mark's approach to community life.

The investigations of Mark's use of the Old Testament in developing his Christology by Marcus, Schneck, and Watts provide a timely reminder about the importance of attending to the Jewish character and background of this Gospel. In many respects Mark's Gospel is a Jewish book. The main characters are Jews; the plot unfolds almost entirely in the land of Israel; and the Scriptures of Israel are put forward as authoritative texts from Jesus' emergence on the public scene (1:2–3) to his death on the cross (15:34).

4
Historical Studies

One of the major concerns of Markan scholarship in the late 1960s and in the 1970s was the attempt to clarify the historical setting in which the Gospel was composed. Then there was a tendency to move Mark eastward, out of the traditional Roman setting, to Galilee or southern Syria. There was also a tendency to postulate a series of theological crises centered on understanding Jesus as primarily a miracle worker or "divine man," and to find in Mark's sometimes negative portrayal of Jesus' disciples a critique of the leaders of the church in Jerusalem. Recent scholarship on Mark has generally abandoned the hypotheses about Mark's corrective Christology and his polemic against the disciples. However, the debate about the Gospel's place of origin remains.

While the Old Testament remains the most obvious background literature for interpreting Mark's Gospel, scholars in recent times have widened their search for parallels to include many kinds of Greco-Roman literature. Besides clarifying the historical context (what was "in the air") of an ancient writing such as Mark's Gospel, historians also have tried to reconstruct the events and developments behind the written text and to discern what sources the writer might have had access to in his work of composition. Finally, the claim that a fragment of Mark's Gospel was found among the Dead Sea scrolls discovered at

Qumran (7Q5) has been revived with great fanfare in recent years, only to be widely rejected once more.

The Setting of the Gospel's Composition

One of the major endeavors in modern Markan studies has been delineating the historical setting in which the Gospel was composed and the specific community in or for which it was written. Mark's Gospel has traditionally (since patristic times) been associated with Rome in the shadow of Nero's persecution of the Christian community there in the late 60s of the first century CE. In recent times, however, there has been a tendency among some Markan interpreters to look eastward and to situate the Gospel's composition in Galilee or southern Syria. The lively debate in the last generation about the place and date of the Gospel's composition was summarized by Frank Matera (1987) on pp. 1–17. Most scholars today date it around 70 CE and place it either at Rome (the traditional place) or some place in Syria or Palestine (the new contender). Two essays by eminent Markan specialists show that the debate continues.

In "The Jewish War and the *Sitz im Leben* of Mark," which appeared in the *Journal of Biblical Literature* (1992), **Joel Marcus** argues that Mark's Gospel reflects the pervasive influence of the First Jewish Revolt (66–74 CE), an event to which the Markan community stood in both geographical and temporal proximity. This setting is indicated by the *ex eventu* prophecies of Mark 13, the description of the Jerusalem temple as a "den of brigands" (11:17), and the treatment of Davidic messianism in various texts (10:46–52, 11:10–11, 12:35–37). According to Marcus, Mark's Gospel was written shortly after 70 CE, perhaps in one of the Hellenistic cities of Palestine. Mainly on the basis of the explanatory parenthesis in Mark 7:3–4 about Jewish customs of handwashing, Marcus views the Markan community as largely Gentile in its composition.

The life-setting proposed by Marcus does explain the turmoil and ferment that is palpable throughout Mark's Gospel. But that mood can be explained just as well by the traditional Roman setting in the aftermath of Nero's persecution of 64 CE. And if the community were largely Gentile, it is hard to imagine how much these people would have grasped from Mark's Gospel and from his use of the Jewish Scriptures in particular, and also hard to imagine why Mark would have written his Gospel in such a "Jewish" way.

John R. Donahue in "Windows and Mirrors: The Setting of Mark's Gospel," published in *Catholic Biblical Quarterly* (1995), contends that Mark's narrative world takes up the concerns of a Christian community located in Rome after the great fire of 64 CE. That community experienced persecution, brutal executions, and betrayal within families. According to Donahue, three threads that run through Mark's Gospel addressed the trials of the Roman church around 70 CE: the shadow of the cross, opposition to Jesus by powerful leaders, and division among Jesus' followers brought about by suffering.

History Behind the Text

In *A Myth of Innocence: Mark and Christian Origins* (1988), **Burton L. Mack** proposes a full-scale theory of "the origin for the Markan view of Christian origins" (p. 357) in which the Evangelist whom we call Mark is the pivotal figure. Mack locates this Gospel's composition in southern Syria in the 70s CE, in the aftermath of the Jewish War (66–74 CE), as an attempt to situate a Christian community there in its new context vis-à-vis various Jewish and Christian groups. He applies the expression "a myth of innocence" to Mark's Gospel because it "separates those who belong to the righteous kingdom within from those without" (p. 372).

While expressing admiration for Mark's literary genius in bringing together various strands of tradition and in creating some clever and memorable fictions, Mack regards the effects of Mark's literary effort as pernicious both in the first century CE and throughout history. Moreover, Mack judges Mark's Gospel to be inadequate for the present needs of our world and regrets that the "church canonized a remarkably pitiful moment of early Christian condemnation of the world" (p. 376).

In his hypothesis of how Mark's Gospel came to be, Mack combines sociological concepts related to group- and sect-formation and the basic concerns of literary (form, source, and redaction) criticism applied to the Gospels. He assumes that Mark wrote the first Gospel and seems to regard him as something of a literary genius. And he contends that Mark's story had little to do with the historical Jesus but much to do with the recent history of the Jesus movement to which Mark belonged.

Mack describes the historical Jesus as "a rather piquant critic of his social world in general" (p. 124). To his contemporaries Jesus would have looked much like a Cynic philosopher going from place to place and challenging conventional assumptions about happiness and the meaning of life. He taught by symbolic actions and pithy sayings, and proposed an ideal (non-apocalyptic) sphere or community in which the kingship of God was acknowledged and lived out. His challenge was directed not only to Jews but also to all who lived under the oppressive regime of the Roman emperor. The social catalyst for the survival of the Jesus movement was the practice of meals in common.

According to Mack, efforts at preserving and carrying on the movement begun by Jesus took many forms and found expression in various ways in Mark's Gospel. These groups included the itinerants in Galilee (who eventually produced the sayings source Q), the "pillars" in Jerusalem (Peter, James, and John), the family of Jesus (who started in Jerusalem and moved to Transjordan), the "congregation of Israel" (Jewish Christians interested in Jewish issues and in the Jewish "roots" of Jesus), the "synagogue reform" (the Christian contributions to a wider phenomenon in Judaism after 70), and the "Christ cult" (Hellenistic Christians who revered

Jesus as a divine being). These groups produced different traditions and imagined Jesus in different ways: wisdom's child (early Q), the last of the prophets (later Q), a man of power like Moses (miracle chains), an enigmatic teacher (parables), and the authoritative lawyer (pronouncement stories). The "Christ cult" focused on the myth of Jesus' death and resurrection.

What Mark did was to appropriate the Christ myth and link it with the Jesus traditions. In doing so, Mark "created the story that was to give to Christian imagination its sense of a radical and dramatic origin in time" (p. 355). Rejecting the traditional scholarly assessment that there is a solid and substantial historical core within Mark's passion narrative, Mack regards it as largely Mark's own fictional creation based loosely on various Jewish patterns (the Righteous One, the Son of Man, the Suffering Servant, etc.). And because Mark had given up on the real world, Mark overlaid all the Jesus traditions with an apocalyptic worldview that relegated the vindication of Jesus and the movements he generated into the distant future.

The picture of Mark the Evangelist that emerges from Mack's reconstruction of Christian origins is that of "a scholar....[a] reader of texts and a writer of texts...a scribe in the Jesus tradition of the synagogue reform movement" (p. 321). Mack goes on to imagine Mark's Gospel as having been composed "at a desk in a scholar's study lined with texts and open to discourse with other intellectuals....a workshop where a lively traffic in ideas and literary experimentation was the rule for an extended period of time" (pp. 324–25).

While not neglecting the literary dimensions of Mark's Gospel, **Adela Yarbro Collins** in *The Beginning of the Gospel: Probings of Mark in Context* (1992) focuses on the historical context of the Gospel and the process through which it came into being. She relies primarily on the methods of the history of religions and tradition history to shed light on the meaning and significance of Mark.

Yarbro Collins's book consists of five substantial essays prepared in connection with her work on a forthcoming full-scale commentary for the Hermeneia series. In treating the genre of Mark, she reviews various proposals (Gospel, history, life or biography) and argues that it is best viewed as the combination of a realistic historical narrative with an eschatological perspective similar to parts of 1 Enoch and Daniel. In exploring how the Markan miracle stories relate to the issues of human suffering and divine justice, she considers ancient and more recent analogies, and notes the apocalyptic framework in which the Markan miracle stories are set: "The Gospel of Mark portrays the miracles of Jesus both as testimony to his role as an agent of God, sharing in the divine power, and as instances in the struggle between the rule of God and the power of Satan" (p. 57).

From an analysis of the apocalyptic discourse in Mark 13, Yarbro Collins rejects the hypothesis of a written, coherent pre-Markan source but admits that the Evangelist may have used oral traditions handed on in Christian catechesis and perhaps reflecting the teaching of Jesus in order to provide a framework of meaning in a difficult situation. However, in the case of the Markan passion narrative, she contends that within the current form of Mark 14:32—15:39 it is possible to discern a series of incidents that have a pre-Markan connection. She observes that the pre-Markan passion source narrated the death of Jesus in terms of the biblical figure of the suffering just person (see Ps 22; Isa 52:13—53:12; Wisdom 2:12–20), and that its most distinctive theological contribution was to combine the role of the suffering just one with that of the Messiah.

In treating the Markan empty tomb narrative (16:1–8), Yarbro Collins views the account not only as a Markan composition but also as a Markan deduction from the early Christian belief in Jesus' resurrection. In the context of afterlife expectations in antiquity she characterizes Mark's approach to Jesus' resurrection as a "translation" (that is, the transfer of the now-immortal hero to another realm) and traces interest in the empty tomb of Jesus to the importance of the graves of heroes in the Greco-Roman world. In the context of early Judaism, she claims that Mark's approach to Jesus' resurrection is closer to the "physical" notion expressed in 2 Maccabees 7 than to the "heavenly" type promoted in Daniel 12. She concludes that the "translation" of the risen Jesus placed the accent more on Jesus' absence than on his presence.

Is it possible to reconstruct the community behind Mark's Gospel? In *The Origins of Mark: The Markan Community in Current Debate* (2000), **Dwight N. Peterson** has subjected three attempts to critical scrutiny. The main concern of Peterson's work, however, is not simply to point out the methodological failings of these three Markan community reconstructors. Rather, he wants to call into question the whole attempt (which has been very important in modern Gospel studies) at describing the community behind the Gospel and then using that description as the key to interpreting the text. He contends that the hypothetical "Markan community" cannot provide the necessary solid ground on which interpreters can stand to read Mark aright because the Markan community is the product of "highly speculative, viciously circular and ultimately unpersuasive and inconclusive reading" (p. 196). Peterson uses three reconstructed Markan communities—based on redaction-critical (Werner Kelber), sociological (Howard C. Kee), and political (Ched Myers) considerations—to show how the whole attempt fails to deliver what it promises.

Taking Mark 13 as his starting point, Kelber in *The Kingdom in Mark: A New Place and New Time* (1974) and *Mark's Story of Jesus* (1979) viewed Mark's Gospel as having been composed in Galilee after 70 CE as a polemic for Mark's northern Christian community against the family of Jesus in the "mother church" in Jerusalem (represented by the "disciples" and the Temple establishment) in a struggle over Christian leadership in the aftermath of the destruction of Jerusalem and its Temple. Peterson accuses Kelber of proceeding in a vicious circle, of treating the Gospel as if it were a Pauline epistle (concerned mainly with present problems in the community) and making it into an allegory, and of oversimplifying the process of delineating the Markan situation.

In *The Community of the New Age: Studies in Mark's Gospel* (1977), Kee located his Markan "apocalyptic" community in southern Syria after the beginning of the Roman-Jewish War in 66 CE but before 70 CE, and used the sociology-of-knowledge approach as developed by Peter Berger to reconstruct the situation behind the Gospel. Kee's interpretive principle, according to Peterson, is legitimation; that is, "if the gospel says it, then the community does it—or in a few cases should do it" (p. 73). Peterson criticizes Kee for too easily assuming that Mark's Gospel is an apocalypse or at least takes over the entire apocalyptic worldview. He also maintains that Kee fails to develop sufficiently his own sociological stance and that he (wrongly) supposes that one can build a historical argument on sociology: "a conjecture dressed up like a sociologist is no less a conjecture" (p. 103).

In *Binding the Strong Man: A Political Reading of Mark's Story of Jesus* (1988), Myers, while claiming that his reading of Mark depends on the historical circumstances surrounding the production of the Gospel, in fact (according to Peterson) let his own life-setting (nonviolent/radical Christian community life with Marxist overtones) determine his interpretive practice. Myers claimed that Mark's Gospel was composed in 69 CE in Galilee in protest against both the Roman imperialistic practices and the oppression under the guise of "religion" perpetrated by those who ran the temple and its political economy. At the same time, Myers claimed that in chapter 13 Mark sought to repudiate the Jewish rebel movement promoting armed resistance and bade his community to maintain their stance of nonviolent resistance in the face of evil coming from all sides. Peterson accuses Myers of circularity in this reconstruction: "Myers' Markan community is really a cipher for his own community, and the ideology he 'discovers' in Mark is in reality the ideology of his own contemporary community" (p. 138). Peterson goes on to argue that Myers did not need to go through the process of "historical reconstruction," since he does not make much constructive use of it. Indeed, Peterson concludes, "far from 'uncovering' the ideology of the text in his reading, Myers has pressed the text of Mark into the service of his own ideological commitments" (p. 149).

Thus, through critical scrutiny of these three attempts, Peterson calls into question the whole enterprise of reconstructing the Markan community solely by means of the Gospel text and then interpreting Mark in light of this so-called community.

In *Hearing the Whole Story: The Politics of Plot in Mark's Gospel* (2001), **Richard A. Horsley** interprets Mark's Gospel, the early Jesus movement, and Jesus himself against the background of village life in Galilee in the first century. He argues that the dominant conflict in Mark's story of Jesus was the political-religious opposition between Jesus and the Roman and Jewish leaders based in Jerusalem. His work combines literary analysis, social history, and the social sciences, and seeks to read the theological elements in Mark from a fresh sociopolitical perspective. His basic goal is delineating the life-setting of Mark's Gospel, and the Jesus whose story it tells.

After insisting that Mark's Gospel be read as a story that is both paradoxical and political, Horsley proposes that the original audience for Mark's story consisted of village communities of a Jesus movement in areas around Galilee, and that its goal was to give guidance and voice to these subject ("submerged") people. Since most of these Galilean village people were not literate, Mark intended that his "text" would be performed orally. In the plot of his story, Jesus and his program of renewing the people of Israel (plus other peoples) in their village communities struggled against the encroachment of the Roman rulers and their Jewish high-priestly collaborators.

Horsley explains the ambiguous portrayal of Jesus' disciples in Mark by taking the Twelve both as representative figures of Israel undergoing renewal and as envoys commissioned to expand Jesus' program of renewal in village communities. In

Jesus' renewal movement the coming of God's kingdom meant that God would rule Israel directly in its village communities, and that "not only would the Romans have to go back into the sea from whence they came, but Israel would have to come directly under the rule of God, as under the traditional Mosaic covenant, freed of oppressive ruling institutions and rulers in its capital" (p. 117). This is what Horsley means when he calls Mark a political text. In fact, he even goes so far as to compare Mark's Jesus to modern "Islamic/Muslim 'fundamentalists'" (p. 43).

Unlike the Jewish apocalyptists who viewed Israel's renewal as almost entirely in the future, Mark's story of Jesus focuses on the presence and imminence of God's kingdom. The apocalyptic discourse in Mark 13 and the exorcisms are viewed by Horsley as symbolic ways of talking about the political struggle against the Roman oppressors and their Jewish collaborators, as the identification of the demon(s) in Mark 5:9 as "Legion" suggests.

In this struggle various groups associated with the Jerusalem temple-state—chief priests, scribes, Sadducees, and Pharisees—have been co-opted. Their attempt to impose a "colonial" program on Galilean village people explains much of the Markan Jesus' resistance to their teachings. Thus it is possible to read Mark 10 and related texts as Jesus' "renewed covenantal 'charter' that lays down teaching on the fundamental matters of marriage and family, economic relations, and the political relations in his movement" (p. 201). In this context the women characters are representative and exemplary: the twelve-year-old girl and the woman with the flow of blood for twelve years (5:21–43) as symbols of Israel in desperate condition, the Syrophoenician woman (7:24–30) as representative of non-Israelites who became part of the Jesus movement, the poor widow (12:41–44) as a pathetic victim of the temple-establishment, and so forth.

Rather than dealing in the theological abstraction of "Christology," Horsley prefers to speak in terms of "scripts." The Markan Jesus generally follows the prophetic script attached to Moses and Elijah, and to a lesser extent the messianic script attached to David.

In the political plot of Mark's Gospel, Jesus appears as the agent for delivering God's people from oppression by their rulers, and for bringing about their restoration and renewal.

Sources Behind the Text

The relationship between Mark's Gospel and John's Gospel has been an object of much debate. There are many obvious similarities between the two texts. But it has always been difficult to prove the direct dependence of one upon the other. Most scholars today regard them as reflecting independent traditions within early Christianity, and explain the similarities as due to the subject matter or to some intersections between the traditions.

In *The Quest of the Historical Gospel: Mark, John, and the Origins of the Gospel Genre* (1997), **Lawrence M. Wills** makes some fresh proposals about Mark's literary genre and about his sources and relationship to John's Gospel. First Wills contends that Mark's Gospel as well as John's Gospel and the *Life of Aesop* (whose extant versions come from the first century; Wills provides a full translation on pp. 181–215) all represent the same literary genre: the aretalogical biography—an account of the great deeds of a god or hero, which is attached to a cult. He also argues that these works (and perhaps others) develop the same theme of the opposition of the protagonist to his people (and perhaps to his god, or at least to his temple), the antagonism that results from this opposition, and the resolution of this antagonism through an expiatory death. The aretalogical biography, according to Wills, is associated with the cult of the dead hero (Jesus in Mark's case). *The Life of Aesop,* though satirical and fictional, is much like Mark and John in telling the story that establishes a cult.

The second major thesis that Wills puts forward is that both Mark and John made use of an older Gospel narrative tradition, and that neither canonical Evangelist was aware of the other's composition. In developing this thesis Wills places the relevant

texts from Mark and John in parallel columns in three large seg-
ments: Mark 1:1—3:30/John 1:1—7:20; Mark 5:21—10:52/John
4:46—11:57; and Mark 11:1—16:20/John 12:12—20:23. As he
treats each parallel passage, Wills provides a detailed commentary
that establishes the similarities, explains what they contribute to
the aretalogical biography, and argues that the Evangelists made
independent use of their common narrative source. He reconstructs the common narrative source in an analytical process much
like that applied to the parallel sayings in Matthew and Luke and
used to reconstruct the sayings source Q. Wills concludes that the
Gospel genre represented by Mark, John, and their common
source arose "as a fluid, often-copied, entertaining prose narrative
used to tell the 'charter myth' of the foundation of the group" (p.
179). While in competing with the lives of other sages Mark (and
John) spoke to a broad social world, in justifying the beginnings of
a worshiping community he spoke to his own social world.

The text of Mark's Gospel that we now possess was written
in Greek around 70 CE and appears to address a mixed readership of Jewish and Gentile Christians, perhaps at Rome or in
Galilee or Syria. But it is generally (and correctly) assumed that
Jesus spoke Aramaic and his earliest disciples were Jews who
lived in the land of Israel around 30 CE. In his *Aramaic Sources
of Mark's Gospel* (1998), **Maurice Casey** sought to devise and
illustrate a method for getting behind the Greek text of Mark to
recover at least some parts of the earliest Aramaic sources of the
Jesus tradition in Mark.

After a sweeping critique of previous efforts at carrying out
this kind of project, Casey contends that real progress is now
possible due primarily to the availability of all the Dead Sea
scrolls written in Aramaic. These manuscripts enable us to know
better than ever before more precisely what Aramaic vocabulary
and syntax were in use in the time of Jesus, and so they provide
the basis from which researchers now can consult earlier and
later forms of Aramaic in their reconstructions of Jesus' words
and deeds.

The goal of Casey's project is the reconstruction of the Aramaic sources rather than simply the retroversion or translation of the Greek text of Mark into Aramaic. This is a critical distinction, because it means that one must stand back from the Greek text and discern how an Aramaic speaker might formulate this idea or describe that activity. One must also be on the lookout for overly literal and thus awkward translations (as leads to be pursued) and signs of deliberate literary or theological editing by the Greek Gospel writers (as elements to be set aside). Basic to Casey's undertaking is the effort to be sensitive to the perspectives of both first-century Palestinian Jews and the ancient translator(s) moving from Aramaic to Greek.

Casey's methodology is illustrated by detailed reconstructions of the Aramaic sources of four passages in Mark's Gospel: Jesus' scriptural understanding of John the Baptist's death (9:11–13); two Sabbath controversies (2:23—3:6); the question of Jacob (= James) and John (10:35–45); and Jesus' final Passover with his disciples (14:12–26). A recurrent expression in these texts is "son of man," which Casey takes as most basically an Aramaic expression for "human" or "man" used by Jesus to refer to himself and also to John the Baptist. And so in the Aramaic sources of Mark 9:11–13 Jesus is said to be referring to John the Baptist as a "son of man" taking on the role attributed to Elijah in Malachi 3:23; Jesus is also said to be applying to John various biblical texts that describe suffering and rejection as the lot of humankind (as in Isa 40:6–8; Job 14; and Jeremiah 6–7). Thus Casey reconstructs Jesus' saying in Mark 9:12 as follows: "Elijah comes first and turns back all, and how it is written of (a/the son) man that he suffers much and is rejected!"

From his reconstructions Casey draws the wide-ranging conclusions that the Greek version of Mark depends on Aramaic sources written by a Jew (or Jews) in the land of Israel before 40 CE, that the Jesus they portray was thoroughly Jewish and even more at home in first-century Palestine than the Greek Gospels describe him as being, and that the Greek version of Mark was revised by

Matthew and Luke in part at least to smooth over some of the perceived awkwardness involved in the translator's moving from Aramaic to Greek. If there is a theological agenda behind Casey's work,
it seems to be the need to recover the words and deeds of Jesus in
their most original and pristine form, and thus to rescue him as a
first-century Palestinian Jew from the distortions brought about by
early Christians and by the Evangelists in particular.

From the middle of the nineteenth century onward, more
and more New Testament scholars have come to assume that
Mark was the first Gospel, and that Matthew and Luke represent
independently revised versions of Mark with expansions from the
sayings source Q and other traditions special to each Gospel (des-
ignated as M and L, respectively). While there have always been
dissident voices and much more complicated theories, the two-
source theory has won the day if for no other reason than its sim-
plicity and economy in explaining most of the evidence. Almost
all the books covered in this volume take the two-source theory as
an assumption.

With regard to relationships among the Synoptic Gospels,
the persistent problem with the two-source theory has been the
presence of many "minor agreements" between Matthew and
Luke over against Mark. While some of these agreements can be
explained in terms of "great minds think alike," such anomalies
ought not to exist in the numbers that they do if, in fact, Matthew
and Luke worked independently with Mark and Q as their primary sources. Some scholars have solved this problem by suggesting that Matthew and Luke worked from an earlier
(Urmarkus) or a later *(Deuteromarkus)* version of Mark's Gospel
than the one now included in our standard editions of the Greek
New Testament text.

In *One Gospel from Two: Mark's Use of Matthew and Luke*
(2002), a team of scholars (**David Peabody, Allan J. McNicol,**
and **Lamar Cope**), which was initially led by the late William R.
Farmer, offers a more radical (though thoroughly traditional) and
far-reaching explanation. Depending in part on Augustine, they

argue that Mark was not the earliest, primitive, foundational Gospel of the church, but rather a carefully composed revision or conflation of its predecessors, Matthew and Luke. The body of their book is a detailed commentary on Mark's Gospel based on this assumption. The team shows that in the order of pericopes Mark alternately agrees with Matthew and Luke, and that within pericopes Mark also often alternately agrees with Matthew and Luke in wording. Moreover, the team contends that the network of repeated words and phrases that are both characteristic of the author of Mark and unique or distinctive within that Gospel reflects a literary, historical, theological, and/or ethical integrity that is consistent with the work of a single author. They even explain Mark's fragmented versions of scriptural arguments in comparison with Matthew's better organized argumentation as evidence for Markan editing. And they claim that their view of Synoptic Gospel relationships is more in keeping with the patristic evidence than the two-source theory is.

Where, when, and why did Mark combine Matthew and Luke into a single Gospel? The team locates Mark's conflation at Rome toward the end of the first century CE for a community that was preoccupied with internal struggles and marginalization at the hands of the wider culture (rather than the issue of the church's relationship to Judaism that had earlier preoccupied Matthew and Luke). Drawing on the Lukan representation of the kerygma of Peter and Paul, Mark recounted the story of Jesus as "the word" or gospel. He has Jesus' opponents function as transparencies of those who marginalized the church in Mark's own time and has the disciples function as transparencies of church leaders and believers in local Christian communities. In this situation Mark's story of Jesus was intended to show how Jesus' life embodied the true nature of the kingdom, and to remind wavering believers that in their marginalization they follow the path of Jesus. From this analysis Mark emerges as an Evangelist with a distinctive perspective and as "clearly the best storyteller among the Gospel writers" (p. 346).

In producing a full-scale commentary on Mark that is based on the "two Gospels into one" model, the team has done what their opponents have frequently challenged them to do. What their commentary shows at the very least is that many of the arguments associated with "solving" the Synoptic Problem (the relationships among Matthew, Mark, and Luke) are reversible. For example, where proponents of the two-source theory see Matthew 12:1–8 as a revision and as strengthening the somewhat clumsy text in Mark 2:23–28, the team explains the Markan version as an example of purposeful Markan redaction.

There are, of course, two major problems with this approach. The first is that the general impression of the Evangelist that emerges is very much like Augustine's unflattering description of Mark as primarily a follower, lackey, and digester of Matthew (*De consensu evangelistarum* 1.2.4) that led to the neglect of Mark until well into the nineteenth century. And secondly, why Mark chose to omit the infancy narratives, the Sermon on the Mount, the special material in the Lukan journey narrative (with its parables of the Good Samaritan and the Prodigal Son), and the resurrection appearance accounts remains hard to explain.

Mark at Qumran?

Has part of Mark's Gospel been discovered among the Dead Sea scrolls? In a series of articles beginning with "¿Papiros neotestamentarios en la cueva 7 de Qumran?" in *Biblica* (1972), the Spanish Jesuit papyrologist **Jose O'Callaghan** proposed that some of the tiny Greek fragments discovered in Qumran Cave 7 in 1955 and published in *Discoveries in the Judaean Desert* III in 1962 are best identified as texts from the Greek New Testament. The most extensive and important example was 7Q5, which O'Callaghan identified as Mark 6:52–53. To do so, he had to diverge from the standard editions of the Greek New Testament. Thus he read *autoi* as *autōn,* equated *tau* and *delta* to yield *diaperasantes,* and omitted *epi tēn* *gēn* to preserve the stichometry. Following the judgment of C. H. Roberts, O'Callaghan dated 7Q5 to ca. 50 CE. Thus 7Q5 (along with other Qumran Cave 7 New Testament texts) would be the earliest extant fragment of the Greek NT.

Some hailed O'Callaghan's identifications as revolutionary, while others counseled caution. Several distinguished scholars (Pierre Benoit, Maurice Baillet, Roberts, Kurt Aland, Gordon D. Fee, etc.) were sharply critical, and so the controversy seemed to be over rather quickly. In the mid-1980s, however, **Carsten Peter Thiede** revived O'Callaghan's proposal and promoted the "New Testament at Qumran" thesis with great zeal in many publications, some intended for the general public and others in scholarly journals.

In *The Earliest Gospel Manuscript? The Qumran Papyrus 7Q5 and Its Significance for New Testament Studies* (1992), Thiede defended O'Callaghan against his critics and argued that his identification of 7Q5 as Mark 6:52–53 was so convincing that future editions of the Greek New Testament should include 7Q5 as a witness to the text of Mark's Gospel. He also contended that since the Qumran caves were closed in 68 CE in the face of Roman attackers and since the script of 7Q5 had been dated independently from 50 BCE to 50 CE, the identification of the text as Mark 6:52–53 would set the composition of Mark's Gospel back to the middle of the first century CE.

Thiede also offered several scenarios to explain how 7Q5 (= Mark 6:52–53) and other New Testament fragments might have come to Qumran before 68 CE. His first explanation was that there were close links between Christians and Essenes in Jerusalem. So when the Christians fled Jerusalem for Pella before the Roman attack, they may have given over for safekeeping some of their sacred texts to Essenes, who in turn brought them to Qumran. Another possibility is that these texts were obtained or even swapped by a Christian missionary for some Essene texts, while a third possibility is that they were simply brought from Jerusalem and stored at Qumran (like other Jewish texts) in the hope that they would escape destruction by the Romans. Whichever explanation one picks, the effect of Thiede's scenarios is to push back the composition of Mark's Gospel to a time earlier than the "around 70 CE" that has become customary among Markan scholars.

However, in *Kein Markustext in Qumran: Eine Unter-suchung der These: Qumran-Fragment 7Q5 = Mk 6, 52–53* (1999), **Stefan Enste** provides a comprehensive critical review of the O'Callaghan-Thiede proposal regarding 7Q5, and argues that the identification of 7Q5 as Mark 6:52–53 is incorrect and based mainly on wishful thinking. After a description of 7Q5, Enste presents a survey of research on the text, takes up the relevance of 7Q5 for dating Mark's Gospel, examines the arguments for and against identifying 7Q5 as Mark 6:52–53, and concludes that 7Q5 = Mark 6:52–53 identification is not only not proved but also highly unlikely.

In the course of his presentation, Enste develops eleven arguments against the 7Q5 = Mark 6:52–53 proposal:

1. The proposal involves an unwarranted equation of *tau* and *delta* to obtain *diasperasantes* in line 3.
2. The space before *kai* in line 3 is misinterpreted as a "paragraph" marker separating Mark 6:52 and 53.
3. A proper stichometry is arrived at only by omitting *epi tēn gēn* in Mark 6:53.
4. The proposal unjustifiably appeals to links and breaks between letters.
5. The paleographical dating proposed by C. H. Roberts was between 50 BCE and 50 CE, with a preference for the first century BC.
6. Given everything that is known about the Qumran group from the other texts found there, it is highly unlikely that New Testament texts would have been preserved at Qumran.

7. The earliest New Testament texts were preserved in the codex format, not on scrolls as 7Q5 seems to have been.
8. Computer-assisted research on the texts has not confirmed the identification.
9. The textual omission of *epi tēn gēn* in Mark 6:53 is unlikely, while its presence destroys the stichometry needed for identifying 7Q5 as Mark 6:52–53.
10. The substitution of *tiaperasantes* for *diaperasantes* cannot be justified.
11. The reading *autōn* for *autoi* (where *iota* is an adscript) is impossible.

Enste has performed a good service in providing a full dossier of a debate that has gone on for some thirty years and in exposing the weaknesses of the 7Q5 = Mark 6:52–53 hypothesis that has been the foundation for the broader "New Testament at Qumran" hypothesis. In most cases he takes up arguments adduced by scholars in the 1970s. But he presents them as part of a comprehensive critique, and especially in response to Thiede's ongoing efforts to promote and expand the hypothesis. He refrains from proposing an alternative identification, though several have been proposed (e.g., Zech 7:4–5; 1 Enoch 15:9d–10), and observes that 7Q5 may be part of a hitherto unknown text. His real purpose is to expose the weakness of the 7Q5 = Mark 6:52–53 hypothesis, and he has succeeded in confirming the general scholarly opinion that this identification is highly unlikely.

Conclusion

If the greatest progress has been made in recent years in studying the literary features and theological message of Mark's Gospel, the progress in historical studies has been much less obvious. Whereas the previous generation focused on the world behind Mark's text and produced many exciting and adventurous theories about it, this generation has focused more on the text itself. Indeed, it was largely out of discontent with the conflicting and confusing "historical" hypotheses put forward by earlier scholars that the shift to the text itself has come to dominate in Markan research.

There is still no consensus about the precise date (beyond "around 70 CE") and place (Rome versus Galilee or southern Syria) of the Gospel's composition. In the effort to find proper comparative materials from the ancient world, more attention has been given to Greco-Roman romances (novels) and rhetorical treatises, with some slighting of Jewish texts. While scholars such as Mack and Horsley have produced elaborate (and quite different) descriptions of the circumstances behind the Gospel's composition, Peterson has cast methodological doubt on the project of writing the history of the Markan community on the basis of the text we have.

On the matter of sources, the proposals about the common source (shared with John) reconstructed by Wills and the Aramaic source reconstructed by Casey, however intriguing they may be, need more testing. The challenge to Markan priority and to the classic two-source theory will probably not convince many scholars, primarily because it is hard to imagine why anyone would write a book like Mark's Gospel on the basis of Matthew and Luke.

5
Engaged Readings

It is possible to read and admire Mark's Gospel as a sophisticated piece of literature, as a source for the basic theological concepts of the early Christian movement, or as a witness to Jewish history in the late Second Temple period and to life within the Roman empire. However, the majority of those who read Mark's Gospel come to it expecting to find spiritual enlightenment and nourishment. It is not surprising then that modern Markan research has generated many "engaged" readings; that is, careful interpretations that explore the Gospel for consolation and challenge on the personal and communal levels.

Perhaps the most surprising development along these lines comes from those who interpret Mark as a "feminist" and/or "political" text, as a book that calls into question assumptions about power, social status, wealth and poverty, and gender in antiquity and today. Mark's Gospel has also become increasingly prominent among those whose interests are Christian spirituality and preaching. The place now given to Mark in the Sunday lectionaries (Year B) in Catholic and mainline Protestant churches has led to the discovery of Mark's Gospel as a precious resource in Christian life.

Feminist Readings

The woman with the flow of blood is one of the most memorable minor characters in Mark's Gospel. **Marla J. Selvidge** in *Woman, Cult, and Miracle Recital: A Redactional Critical Investigation on Mark 5:24–34* (1990) contends that this passage (commonly known as "the healing of the woman with the flow of blood") preserves a miracle story that freed women from restrictive cultic and social roles, and freed them to take up new, demanding, creative, and healing roles within the Markan community.

After noting that the academic community has recently rediscovered the positive and liberating side of Mark 5:24–34, Selvidge argues that most of Mark's first auditors/readers were dissident, anti-Twelve, and cosmopolitan, and therefore open to leadership possibilities found within the women of the Christian community. She suggests that this miracle story was preserved as a definitive answer to the biblical purity laws (especially in Leviticus) that historically had attempted to control women in their cultic and social expressions within the Jewish community. This situation stands in contrast to what prevailed in the Greco-Roman world. There women had relative freedom in cultic activities and were not prohibited from accepting responsibility in cults because of their gender or their menstrual cycle in particular.

In Mark 5:24–34, the woman with the flow of blood takes the initiative, circumvents the established system of Jewish purity rules, and heads toward Jesus as a "god-figure." According to Selvidge, this woman stands as a bulwark of faith, an example of faith healing, a proclaimer of truth, and a genuine servant, as she lives out the roles of following, suffering, and denying: "Where the twelve fail, the woman succeeds" (p. 107). As a person who could experience and intelligibly discern the presence of God, this woman could participate in Christian religious activities and serve as a communicator in the community. She perceived, recognized, and understood the voice of God, and so she exhibited the kind of faithful life needed by the emerging Christian communities. Thus, the woman with the flow of blood emerges as an exemplar for women (and men) in the Markan community, and provides another clue about the prominence of woman in early Christianity. Using a critical rhetorical approach to selected texts in Mark's Gospel, **Hisako Kinukawa** in *Women and Jesus in Mark: A Japanese Feminist Perspective* (1994) examines the interactions between women and Jesus, with particular attention to how boundary-breaking activity changes and enriches both characters. The context in which Kinukawa reads these texts is the patriarchal and hierarchical society found both in first-century Palestine and in Japan throughout history and into modern times. These two societies have a culture of honor and shame, with its strong sense of group-oriented consciousness, dyadic personality, and gender-role difference. She notes that in these cultures "women have been subordinated to bear all the shame of society so that men can seek honor" (p. 29).

The Markan interactions between women and Jesus are quite positive, and serve to reveal him as life-giving and his "good news" as liberating for women and threatening at least to some men. Kinukawa concludes that the "women in Mark invite us to overcome the barriers from our side so that we may experience life-communion with Jesus" (p. 144). The combination of perspectives that Kinukawa brings to the texts—critical rhetorical, Japanese, and feminist—help her to bring fresh insights to Jesus' interactions with women according to Mark. And her focus on the mutual transformations undergone by both Jesus and the women makes for an interesting contribution to the study of Christology and discipleship in the Gospel.

Against this background the hemorrhaging woman in Mark 5:25–34 appears as an outcast from the perspectives of physical malady, social status, and religious purity rules. By taking the initiative she reaches out to Jesus by touching him and her malady is healed. Her breaking of boundaries and Jesus' compassionate reception of it restore her to wholeness on various levels. Likewise, the Syrophoenician woman in Mark 7:24–30—a female, a foreigner, and one "unclean" by both birth and contact with her daughter's demon—risks everything on her encounter with Jesus and brings about a mutual transformation along with the physical healing.

The generosity shown by the poor widow in Mark 12:41–44 is taken by Kinukawa as heightening Jesus' impatience with the Jerusalem temple system and inspiring him to move toward his own collision with power. The anointing woman of Mark 14:3–9 emerges as the first person to recognize Jesus' certain death and the significance of that event. The women disciples at the cross (Mark 15:40–41, 47; 16:1) illustrate that Jesus' universal call "to follow" actually entails "serving" in the sense of life-giving suffering. Even Jesus' strict teachings about divorce and adultery in Mark 10:1–12 help to protect the rights of women and to promote their equality with men. An excellent collection of essays on women in Mark's Gospel has been edited by Amy-Jill Levine and appears under the title *A Feminist Companion to Mark* (2001).

Joan L. Mitchell in *Beyond Fear and Silence: A Feminist-Literary Reading of Mark* (New York: Continuum, 2001) takes Mark 16:8 as the key to understanding and interpreting the Gospel as a whole. It is now widely accepted among New Testament scholars that Mark's Gospel originally ended with16:8, with the three women—Mary Magdalene, Mary the mother of James and Joses, and Salome—who on Easter Sunday morning visited Jesus' tomb, found it empty, and fled. Their flight is described in the following way: "terror and amazement had seized them; and they said nothing to anyone, for they were afraid." These women saw Jesus die, knew where he was buried, and came to the tomb only to be told by "a young man" that Jesus "has been raised; he is not here" (16:6). Mark 16:8 is puzzling on two counts: the reaction of the women ("terror and amazement"), and their apparent failure to convey the message about the empty tomb and Jesus' resurrection.

Rather than being put off by these apparent puzzles, Mitchell notes that Mark deliberately characterizes Jesus' first followers, both men and women, as frequently afraid and amazed beyond words. She also observes that Mark does not say that the women never tell the good news that Jesus is risen. Rather, their silence is temporary (otherwise the news would never have gotten out) and echoes Jesus' own silence during the passion. Instead of a narrative about the women delivering the message or about appearances of the risen Jesus, the real ending of Mark's Gospel is in the response of its hearers/readers. Its open-ended character deliberately invites responses and dialogue.

Mitchell employs a model of feminist biblical interpretation developed by Elisabeth Schüssler Fiorenza. The first step in this model involves applying the hermeneutic of suspicion: "Suspect androcentric and patriarchal biases in the passage." In the case of Mark 16:8 the suspicion falls not so much on Mark the Evangelist as it does on those who added the various longer "endings" to Mark's text and the other Evangelists who by including appearance stories showed themselves to be either insensitive to or dissatisfied with Mark's literary and theological subtlety. But Mark himself is guilty of covering over the active role played by women disciples in Jesus' public ministry; he reveals it only in 15:41, near the end of his narrative: "These used to follow him and provided for him when he was in Galilee; and there were many other women who had come up with him to Jerusalem."

The second step in Mitchell's project is to "reconstruct the passage historically with the women at the center rather than at the margin." At the level of Jesus' public ministry around 30 CE, passages such as Mark 15:40–41, 47, and 16:1–8, as well as other Markan texts about the women, indicate that women played significant roles in the earliest Jesus movement. The message about Jesus' empty tomb and resurrection did get out enough to bring the church into existence, and the women witnesses very likely played roles analogous or even equal to that of the male disciples like Peter. When Mark's Gospel was being composed around 70 CE, the members of the first Christian generation, male and female alike, were dying off. Mark wrote his Gospel to convince the next generation of Christians to take up the task of getting out the message concerning Jesus' life, death, and resurrection. The women are portrayed in Mark's Gospel as authentic disciples of Jesus, as Mark 15:41 makes clear. Their response to the empty tomb is one of religious awe or numinous fear. Their silence is rooted in the silence of Jesus and his male disciples throughout the Gospel. It is a holy silence in the face of divine revelation and the commitment it evokes.

The third and fourth steps involve proclaiming the relevant Markan passages and using our voices to let the Markan women speak. Here Mitchell suggests that Mark's Gospel provides today's communities of reception with both a summons to dialogue in 16:8 and a model of emancipatory dialogue in the conversation between Jesus and the Syrophoenician woman (7:24–30). She concludes that "in their silence in Mark 16:8b, the three women disciples are midwives of the birth of Jesus' word into story....In our foremothers' silence, the narrative still calls the disciples of the next generation to speak for themselves and bring the gospel into dialogue with their lives" (p. 115).

Political Readings

Ched Myers's *Binding the Strong Man: A Political Reading of Mark's Story of Jesus* (1988) takes its title from Jesus' parable in Mark 3:27: "No one can enter a strong man's house and plunder his goods unless they first bind the strong man; then indeed they may plunder his house." Myers's political reading of Mark's Gospel is not so much a verse-by-verse commentary as an "episode-by-episode" exposition, studying the meaning of each literary unit and its relationship to the other units and to the overall ideological strategy of Mark. He approaches Mark's story of Jesus (written in Galilee around 69 CE) as an ideological narrative, the manifesto of an early Christian discipleship community in its war of myths with the dominant social order and its political adversaries.

In describing his own political perspective, Myers places himself on the side of the Marxist tradition with regard to the theory of ideology, the task of ideological criticism, and a conflict model of society. However, he contends that the biblical narrative of liberation is the source of what may be good in Marxism. Writing against the background of "Ronald Reagan's American empire," Myers identifies himself with the Christian movement of "radical discipleship."

Myers focuses on Mark's Gospel because it is "a narrative for and about the common people" (p. 39) insofar as it reflects the daily realities of disease, poverty, and disenfranchisement that characterized the social existence of first-century Palestine's "other 95%." He contends that Mark's Gospel was written in the social and political ferment of the First Jewish Revolt, and that Mark portrayed Jesus as offering a perspective different from those of the Jewish ruling classes, the Roman imperial system, and the Jewish religious reformers and militaristic rebels. In championing Jesus' nonviolent resistance, Mark offered "a grassroots social discourse that is at once both subversive and constructive" (p. 87).

Myers's treatment of his "title" text (Mark 3:27) illustrates concretely his approach to Mark's Gospel. He interprets the parable of the strong man in terms of "the political war of myths" (p. 165). The logic of the scribes' charge against Jesus is that since the scribes believed themselves to be God's representatives, Jesus' secession necessarily put him in allegiance to Satan. But Jesus short-circuits their self-serving ideological dualism by unmasking its contradictions and collapsing it upon itself. In 3:27 Jesus places the scribes on Satan's side in the political struggle, and suggests that he as the "stronger one" heralded by John the Baptist (1:8) intends to overthrow the reign of the strong man (the scribal establishment represented by the demon of 1:24). With this parable Jesus claims that the scribes are aligned with Satan against God's purposes. However, with the "Amen" saying in

3:28, Jesus offers a blanket pardon except for those who (like the scribes) mistake the work of the Holy Spirit for that of Satan.

On the larger scale, Myers's political approach comes out in titles that he gives to various parts of Mark's Gospel: "direct action campaign" (1:21—3:35, 11:1—13:3); "sermon on revolutionary patience" (4:1–34, 13:4–37); "construction of a new social order" (4:35—8:9); and "Jesus' arrest and trial by the powers" (14:1—15:20).

Myers concludes that Mark "called for resistance to the rule of the 'strong man,' and the creation of a new world: a practice of revolutionary discipleship" (p. 421). The key institution for the Markan community was the household, which gave it social stability (over against the Jerusalem temple and the synagogues) and perhaps also served as "the haven for underground activity" (p. 435). Its revolutionary insight was that "the powers could only be defeated by the power of what we today call 'nonviolence'" (p. 446). The lasting message of Mark's Gospel, according to Myers, is that "if Jesus contested the powers through the subversive practice of symbolic direct action, then we must in our context find meaningful and clear ways to do the same" (p. 452).

Herman C. Waetjen's *A Reordering of Power: A Sociopolitical Reading of Mark's Gospel* (1989) takes as its starting point for interpreting the story world of Mark's Gospel and the setting for its composition after 70 CE the agrarian societies of Roman-occupied Palestine and Roman-occupied Syria, respectively. In these agrarian societies land was the primary source of wealth and power, and most of the people (including Jesus and his first followers) were near the bottom of the social pyramid along with peasants, artisans, unclean and degraded persons, and the "expendables."

In this sociopolitical context Jesus emerges at the time of his baptism "in the Jordan" (1:9–11) as "the New Human Being" (Waetjen's rendering of "the Son of Man)." Jesus' baptism by John was an eschatological experience of death, and his subsequent baptism by the Holy Spirit was an eschatological experience of re-creation or resurrection. The baptism ended Jesus' participation in the structures of his Roman and Jewish society, and so he became the bearer of God's sovereignty over the entire creation: "As the New Human Being, he is the ultimate human being, the one who is so completely and perfectly human that the image of God will become transparent in his life and activity" (p. 72).

According to Waetjen, Jesus, once a carpenter but now God's viceregent, will be the artisan whose divinely empowered hands will build a kingdom that will never be destroyed. Through him God's millennial rule is being actualized for the masses of the poor, oppressed, diseased, and dispossessed people of Galilee. Most of Jesus' followers seem to have been displaced persons. At the top of the social pyramid stood the ruling class, oriented toward preserving the existing structures and institutions without regard for the mutuality of interests and obligations that they were supposed to order and supervise.

In his teachings and activities Jesus rejects the myths of Jewish apocalypticism about an imminent cataclysmic divine intervention on the side of Israel or of the righteous within Israel. Rather, for Jesus, God's rule is like the activity of a peasant during an agricultural season (see Mark 4:1–34), a collaboration between peasants and the earth. Jesus opposes the colonialism represented by the Roman "legion" (see 5:9), the tradition-bound Judaism of the temple authorities and the Pharisees, and the violent revolutionary activity of the Zealots. The rule of God that Jesus as the New Human Being is establishing is "a new moral order, horizontal in structure and therefore essentially egalitarian, in which human destiny will be realized both individually and corporately" (p. 145).

The "New Israel" or "New Humanity" founded by Jesus is "the social reality of the one and the many into which all human beings are called" (p. 160). And eternal life is a dynamic state of personal and social existence not controlled by fear of death, and therefore free from alienation and narcissism and their expressions in greed, injustice, exploitation, oppression, dispossession, and living death.

Jesus as "the New Human Being" must die in Jerusalem (the *axis mundi*) to negate the old order of oppression and dispossession. Likewise, he must rise again in Jerusalem to establish the New Humanity that cannot be abolished by the power of the old order. By his death on the cross Jesus becomes the bridge that unites God and humankind. By his resurrection the eschatological reality that Jesus actualized in his deeds and words during his ministry has been reconstituted ontologically. By his exit from the tomb and departure from Jerusalem to Galilee, the divine presence of the New Humanity can be experienced wherever the living temple of the New Humanity is encountered.

Spirituality

In *The Gospel of Mark* (1988), which is part of the series entitled the Message of Biblical Spirituality, **Karen Barta** explores how "as this paradoxical story of Jesus unfolds, our own stories are illumined" (p. 126), and so offers insights regarding spirituality. She notes that Mark's Gospel repeatedly disturbs our sensibilities and shatters our illusions, and that according to Mark crossing boundaries is what faith is all about.

Taking her starting point from the abrupt ending in Mark 16:8 — "and they [the women] said nothing to anyone, for they were afraid" — Barta contends that Mark's Gospel not only destroys false images and deadly illusions but also creates new possibilities. In this framework prayer according to Mark is associated with the wilderness (and not the Jerusalem temple) and takes place in the midst of anger, grief, sadness, and despair. The kingdom of God proclaimed by Mark's Jesus involves a vision of the human community in which even the most powerless and needy are empowered, and in which the king is recognized only in Jesus' condemnation and cruel death on the cross.

The miracles of Jesus take place in contexts of conflict, faith, misunderstanding, and mission. They reveal how Jesus can and does break down external and internal boundaries. The exorcisms, too, are liberation stories about breaking barriers and crossing boundaries (see Mark 5:1–20). Likewise, the healings of the blind men in Mark 8:22–26 and 10:46–52 remind us that the "cure" for intellectual, moral, and religious blindness is conversion. The lesson to be drawn from the various kinds of disciples in Mark—the Twelve, the women, the "minor" characters—is that discipleship is "both open-ended and demanding; it is neither exclusive nor easy" (p. 123). The Gospel taken as a whole reminds us that "the crucified one goes before you; seeing him is a matter of faith. Faith awakens the artist within" (p. 127).

Mark's Gospel is not the whole of biblical spirituality. Nevertheless, as Barta shows convincingly, Mark's Gospel does encompass everything that is human: life and death, joy and grief, success and failure, sickness and health, weakness and strength, suffering and pleasure. And as Barta leads readers through this Gospel, she challenges them to face the great realities that constitute the spiritual life and to appreciate the surprising perspectives that Mark's Gospel brings to them.

Another approach to Mark's contribution to Christian spirituality is represented by **William Reiser** in *Jesus in Solidarity with His People: A Theologian Looks at Mark* (2000). He observes that the theological glue that holds together Mark's many narrative pieces is his unswerving sense of the presence of the risen Jesus. It is from the perspective of Jesus' death and resurrection that Mark portrays Jesus in solidarity with his people, especially with the "throwaways."

Reiser's work is not a commentary or even a full reading of Mark's Gospel. Rather it consists of twelve essays that explore key features of Markan spirituality in the light of biblical exegesis, theological insights, and pastoral sensitivity. While Reiser regards Mark as the first Gospel, he insists that "it is not a beginner's manual but a text for those who have already made some progress along the way of God" (p. 18). He gives particular attention to the theme of Jesus' suffering in solidarity with God's people and what this might mean for those who wish to follow him.

Reiser views the baptism of Jesus not only as a moment of prayer and faith but also as Jesus' point of insertion into the historical drama of human salvation. The total, loving dedication to God above everything else that made Jesus the sinless one is the way of living to which others have been invited. In the renewed Israel Jesus envisioned forgiveness to be a regular and pervasive feature of life and a lifting away of whatever burdens that crush human lives. For Jesus and his followers, doing the will of God means leading a life built on obedience to the Holy Spirit (faith) and serves as the ground of hope.

That the kingdom of God should begin among the world's rejected ones ("throwaways") is a mystery. Indeed, Jesus himself can be described as "the quintessential throwaway." Reiser interprets the controversy about paying taxes to Caesar (Mark 12:13–17) as Jesus' forthright rejection of political pragmatism in favor of a prophetic embrace of covenant faith and trust in God's reign (rather than the emperor's power). The parables challenge the imagination of hearers/readers to harvest the signals that confirm Easter faith, though the fact that some do not "get" them is part of the mysterious dynamics of grace and freedom.

The necessity of suffering in God's plan has to do with the conflict provoked by prophetic living; taking up the cross of Jesus involves taking on oneself the whole project or mission of Jesus. The redemptive suffering of Jesus (see 10:45) allows men and women to recover their freedom. The transfiguration narrative (9:2–8) places Jesus and his followers in the company of prophets (Elijah and Moses) and also with the heavily burdened members of God's people.

Can God be trusted? This is the great question of spirituality and one about which Mark's Gospel challenges us to come to decision. The test case is the death of Jesus on the cross (15:21–39), when Jesus' reliance on Psalm 22 (the whole psalm!)

respects both the reality of his suffering and his trust in God's power to vindicate him in the resurrection. The risen Jesus is to animate, guide, and empower his followers to continue his mission. At the same time, following this Messiah is "to be drawn into his suffering and death, which turn out to be a mirror of the historical fortunes of God's poor....Mark never says that because Jesus suffered his followers would be spared" (p. 204).

Preaching

All over the world the primary vehicle for reading and interpreting Mark's Gospel (or any Gospel) is the Sunday liturgy held in the various Christian churches. One of the most practical and far-reaching developments that emerged from the Second Vatican Council (1962–65) was the adoption of a three-year cycle of readings for all the Sundays of the year. Each year features a different Synoptic Gospel: Matthew in Year A, Mark in Year B, and Luke in Year C. Selections from John's Gospel appear on major feasts (like Christmas Day and Good Friday) and on the Sundays during Lent and the Easter season. The Old Testament reading often serves as "background" for the Gospel reading, and the responsorial psalm provides a "bridge" between the Old Testament and the Gospel texts. The epistle readings (from Romans, 1 Corinthians, etc.) are on a separate (continuous) cycle.

This lectionary schema drawn up originally by and for the Roman Catholic Church was quickly accepted with some modifications by mainline Protestant churches (Anglican, Lutheran, Methodist, Presbyterian, etc.). The revised lectionary gave new prominence to Mark's Gospel, which traditionally had been neglected in favor of Matthew or Luke. So Mark's Gospel now has a year of its own when it is the focus of attention. Year B takes place in 2006, 2009, 2012, and so forth.

There are now available many guides to Mark intended for those who preach, pray on, and discuss (in Bible-study groups) texts from that Gospel. Here I mention only two that seem note-worthy for the scholarship behind them and for their sensitivity to the pastoral needs of people today.

Bonnie Bowman Thurston's *Preaching Mark* (2002) is a running exposition of the whole Gospel. With the needs of preachers in mind, Thurston approaches each pericope with two basic questions: Why did Mark preserve this story? and Why was it important for his community? Adopting what she calls a "hermeneutic of belief," she focuses on Mark's pattern of organi-zation and on the relevance of his Gospel to Christian life today. The result is an excellent short commentary on Mark along with practical suggestions about how preachers and teachers might make connections between individual texts and the problems and possibilities that we face in the twenty-first century. An appendix lists the Gospel readings for Year B according to the lectionaries used in the Roman Catholic and various Protestant churches.

John R. Donahue's *Hearing the Word of God: Reflections on the Sunday Readings: Year B* (2002) takes its lead directly from the Catholic lectionary cycle (First Sunday of Advent, Sec-ond Sunday of Advent, etc.) and offers concise comments on the Markan texts and their connections with the other readings for the day. Donahue has been one of the best Markan scholars for many years, and he brings to the Markan lectionary passages a compre-hensive knowledge of the texts and the scholarship on them. His starting point is often some personal experience or general human experience (sickness, fear, etc.) to which he brings insights that emerge from the Markan and other Sunday biblical texts. Each unit ends with suggestions about "praying with scripture" over the human situations and/or the theological themes evoked by the lectionary passages.

Both Thurston and Donahue offer reliable guides to the liter-ary, historical, and theological interpretation of Mark's Gospel. They also provide fresh insights on how these texts might affect the lives of people today. Their works are good examples of New Tes-tament scholarship bridging the gap between technical scholarship and a general audience today. They exemplify nicely a faith-based reading and interpretation of Mark's Gospel intended to enrich the pastoral mission of the church.

One of the most prominent developments in biblical studies in recent years has been the recognition of the influence of the social location of the interpreter on the interpretation of a text. Who I am and where I am can and do make a difference in how I read a text. *Preaching Mark in Two Voices* (2002) brings together two authors who have much in common. Both are male, American, Protestant, well-educated, alumni of the same university, and so on. **Brian K. Blount** is an associate professor of New Testament at Princeton Theological Seminary, and **Gary K. Charles** is pastor of the Old Presbyterian Meeting House in Alexandria, Virginia. What distinguishes them most with regard to social location in the United States is their race. While Blount draws parallels between Mark's message and his own African-American-church heritage of slavery and oppression, Charles struggles with how to make Mark's disturbing Gospel "good news" for well-educated white suburbanites living on the outskirts of Washington, DC.

In each chapter of their joint treatment of Mark's Gospel, there is an exposition of a large section (1:1—3:6, 3:7–35, 4:1–41, etc.) along with a sermon by the expositor and a reflection/meditation by the other author. One theme that unifies their exegeses and sermons is the boundary-breaking character of Mark's Gospel: "Mark offers a Jesus who embodies and preaches God's boundary-breaking, transformative message for Israel and all humankind" (p. 10). This theme was developed already by Blount in his solo work *Go Preach! Mark's Kingdom Message and the Black Church Today* (1998). There Blount argued that Mark's Gospel offers a narrative presentation of a Jesus whose apocalyptic revelation of God's kingdom shatters the institutions, laws, and codes that structured religious and political society in first-century Palestine.

In their joint work, the section that the authors entitle "A 'Real' Family Reunion (Mark 3:7–35)" begins with Blount's

presentation of the major exegetical issues, with particular attention to the tensions between Jesus' natural family (who regard
Jesus as crazy or even possessed) and his "real" family made up
of persons willing to commit themselves to doing God's will.
Then Blount provides the text of a sermon that he gave at a
reunion of his own family in which he concludes that family is
not about blood or kinship but rather is "about the reign of God
coming and the world of humanity changing so that it can meet
that reign in a right relationship when it gets there" (p. 55). Blount
observes that "Jesus is probably the last person you'd even want
to *invite* to a family reunion" (p. 49). Charles then shows that
Jesus' natural family had problems with him because they were
outsiders to his project, and because Jesus and discipleship can be
best understood only from the inside.

This imaginative book, boundary-breaking in its own right,
shows that biblical exegesis and actualization (in this case,
preaching) need not be kept separate. Rather, it illustrates well the
creative relationship that can exist between the two operations,
and how the interpreter's social location can effect how a text is
read (exegesis) and how it may speak to different audiences or
congregations (actualization).

Commentaries

The commentary is one of the oldest and most familiar vehi-
cles for communicating biblical scholarship. Modern commentaries are expected to analyze books from the perspectives of their
literary features, historical setting, and theology. They are com-
pendiums of past research, syntheses of current study, and point-
ers toward future developments. After an introduction dealing
with basic questions about the book (author, place and date of
composition, genre, purpose, structure, etc.), commentaries typi-
cally provide for each pericope a translation (or assume access to
one already in use), offer notes on the text (regarding language,

textual variants, ancient parallels, etc.), and give an interpretation (with reference to literary structure, historical context, and theological significance).

Until recently Mark's Gospel had been relatively poor in commentaries both in antiquity and in modern times. What patristic comments have come down to us have been selected, translated, and gathered by **Thomas C. Oden** and **Christopher A. Hall** in the *Mark* volume in the Ancient Christian Commentary of Scripture series (1998). The earliest-known commentary on Mark was thought to be from Jerome but more likely was written by an Irish monk in the seventh century; see **Michael Cahill,** *The First Commentary on Mark: An Annotated Translation* (1998). The relative neglect of Mark in patristic times was due to the eclipse of Mark by the revised and expanded versions produced by Matthew and Luke, and by Augustine's negative assessment of Mark as simply a follower, lackey, and digester of Matthew.

The lack of great modern commentaries apart from **Vincent Taylor's** *The Gospel According to Mark* (1952; 2nd ed., 1966) is not so easy to explain. At any rate, the period covered by this survey has seen (especially in recent years) several substantial commentaries on Mark as well as many shorter treatments of the whole Gospel. The six works noted here are representative of what modern commentaries are supposed to do. They provide literary, historical, and theological treatments of Mark's Gospel. But they also generally treat the text from an explicit methodological perspective or angle, and so they illustrate what has been the broader trend in Markan studies over the past twenty years.

Morna D. Hooker's *The Gospel According to Mark* (1991) is the work of a learned Markan scholar that took shape over more than twenty years. In her introduction she traces how the task of the commentator on Mark's Gospel has evolved over the past fifty years from source criticism and source historical context (Vincent Taylor), through form criticism and early church life (Dennis Nineham), to redaction criticism and the distinctive contributions made by the Evangelist (Eduard Schweizer). While not ignoring the concerns of these earlier commentators, Hooker attempts to look at the finished product that we call Mark's Gospel, not simply analyzing individual units, but examining the structure of the book as whole in order to discover, if possible, what lessons the Evangelist was trying to convey to his readers.

Reflecting more explicitly the new literary approaches, **John Paul Heil** in *The Gospel of Mark as a Model for Action: A Reader-Response Commentary* (1992) focuses on each scene and thus ultimately on the whole Gospel as a practical "model for action" for its Christian audience. In a sequential manner Heil presents, explains, and interprets Mark's story of Jesus with special emphasis on the responses of the implied reader to each scene. By considering Mark's dramatic narrative as a dynamic process of communication between author and audience, calling forth definite and active responses applicable to the audience's life, Heil seeks to illuminate the Gospel's meaning and pragmatic value for Christians today. He takes as the dominant theme of Mark's Gospel how the "way" of the Lord God was actualized and executed by the "way" of Jesus.

In his two-volume exposition entitled *The Beginning of the Gospel: Introducing the Gospel According to Mark* (1999), **Eugene LaVerdiere** describes Mark's Gospel as an act of proclamation that made Jesus, the one who was crucified and raised from the dead, present to Mark's readers and listeners. Using literary and rhetorical analysis, LaVerdiere shows how Mark applied the story of Jesus and his first disciples to the early church in his own day, and indicates how this story might be applied to the church at the beginning of the third millennium. LaVerdiere gives particular attention to the symbols of the sea and the bread in Mark 1:1 — 8:21, and to the symbols of the way and the cup in 8:22 — 16:8. Both parts are concerned with asking and answering questions about the identity and mission of Jesus and of the church.

In *Mark 1–8* (2000), **Joel Marcus** gives particular attention to reading Mark's Gospel in its historical context of first-century Judaism and to the implications of the events of 70 CE for Jews and Jewish Christians in the eastern Mediterranean world. He contends that a Syrian provenance around 70 CE is the strongest theory available regarding the place and date of composition for Mark's Gospel, and argues that Mark's narrative is aptly described as promoting an apocalyptic cosmology. He treats the first half of the Gospel under four major headings: prologue (1:1–15); honeymoon and beginning of opposition (1:16—3:6); the intensifying struggle (3:7—6:6a); and feasts (6:6b—8:21). Marcus regards salvation, according to Mark as for other Jewish apocalyptists, as above all a liberation of humanity from the cosmic powers that oppress it, and views Jesus' main mission (including his teaching) to be clearing the earth of demons whose power is made manifest by extension also in the human opposition to Jesus.

The Gospel of Mark: A Commentary (2002) by **Francis J. Moloney** seeks "to marry the rich contribution made by traditional historical scholarship with the contemporary focus on narrative as such" (p. xvii). It also tries to show what Mark's story of Jesus as the suffering Messiah and his failing disciples might say not only to "an early Christian community perplexed by failure and suffering" (p. xviii) but also to Christians today. He inclines toward placing the Gospel's composition in southern Syria between 70 and 75 CE. Thus, Moloney deals with the worlds behind the text, in the text, and before the text. His exposition of Mark is a blend of the old (historical criticism) and the new (narrative analysis) trends in Markan scholarship.

With regard to Mark's literary design, Moloney discerns two major sections (1:14—8:30 and 8:31—15:47). In the first half the Evangelist raises the question, Who is Jesus? And he treats it in terms of Jesus' relationships with Israel (1:14—3:6), his new family (3:7—6:6a), and his disciples (6:6b—8:30). In the second half, according to Moloney, the Evangelist answers the question, saying that Jesus is "the suffering and vindicated Son of Man, the Christ and Son of God" (p. 19). This response is developed during the narratives about the journey of Jesus and his disciples to Jerusalem

(8:31 — 10:52), the various "endings" associated with Jesus' ministry in Jerusalem (11:1 — 13:37), and his passion and death (14:1 — 15:47).

The approach taken by **John R. Donahue** and myself in *The Gospel of Mark* (2002) is characterized as an "intratextual and intertextual reading." The term *intratextuality* here means reading Mark *as* Mark and *by* Mark. Reading Mark as Mark means focusing on the final form of the Gospel text (and not so much on its sources or literary history), focusing on its words and images, literary devices and forms, structures, characters, and plot. Reading Mark by Mark means giving particular attention to the distinctive words and themes that run through the Gospel and hold it together as a unified literary production. "Intertextuality" means noting the links of Mark's Gospel to other ancient texts (especially the Old Testament) and to the life of the Markan community (at Rome around 70 CE) and of the Christian community today.

Conclusion

The "engaged readings" covered in this chapter flow nicely from the literary and theological studies treated in chapters 2 and 3. To varying extents, these books illustrate and foster the process of "actualization"; that is, letting the biblical text address and challenge readers today.

While there are only a few female characters in Mark's narrative and none of them is a major figure, the synthetic work by Kinukawa shows that there is a liberating motif running through the texts that deal with women. While the political readings run the risk of eisegesis (reading into the text), they do bring out the value of attending to the social locations of both the text and of the interpreter, and catch the starkness and challenge of Mark's Gospel.

The books on Markan spirituality by Barta and Reiser bring out the distinctive approach to Christian life represented by Mark among the Gospels and other New Testament writings. The guides to preaching on Mark's Gospel illustrate the application and continuation of solid exegesis to the form in which the text is most commonly read and interpreted. The commentaries, with their distinctive approaches and methodologies made explicit, not only synthesize the work of a new generation of scholars but also indicate the directions in which Markan study has gone and is now going.

The **Pontifical Biblical Commission's** 1993 document on *The Interpretation of the Bible in the Church* called attention to the proliferation of methods being applied to biblical texts today. The variety of approaches to and readings of Mark's Gospel discussed in this book suggest that the search for *the* method of interpretation and *the* meaning of a text will prove increasingly elusive. Rather, now we have multiple methods issuing in multiple readings. The image of a symphony orchestra comes to mind. All the interpreters are using the same text, bringing out different aspects of the text by the instruments that they use, and producing a richer and fuller reading of the text that can add to the reader's comprehension and appreciation.

In the case of Mark's Gospel, it appears that the turn to the text itself and the application of the "new" methods to it have contributed significantly to our appreciation of the inexhaustible riches of this Gospel and of Mark's skill as an author and theologian. The "engaged readings" are proof of the practical and positive value of the "new" methods and confirm the statement made by the Pontifical Biblical Commission: "Exegesis produces its best results when it is carried out in the context of the living faith of the Christian community, which is directed toward the salvation of the entire world" (p. 166).

Bibliography

The page numbers after the entry refer to where that item is treated in this book. The abbreviation JSNT stands for *Journal for the Study of the New Testament.*

Anderson, Janice Capel and Stephen D. Moore, eds. *Mark & Method: New Approaches in Biblical Studies.* Minneapolis: Fortress, 1992. See pp. 7–9.

Barta, Karen. *The Gospel of Mark.* Message of Biblical Spirituality 9. Wilmington, DE: Glazier, 1988. See pp. 78–79.

Beavis, Mary Ann. *Mark's Audience: The Literary and Social Setting of Mark 4.11–12.* JSNT Supplement Series 33. Sheffield, UK: JSOT Press, 1989. See pp. 12–13.

Blount, Brian K. *Go Preach! Mark's Kingdom Message and the Black Church Today.* Maryknoll, NY: Orbis, 1998. See p. 83.

Blount, Brian K. and Gary K. Charles. *Preaching Mark in Two Voices.* Louisville, KY: Westminster John Knox, 2002. See pp. 83–84.

Broadhead, Edward K. *Naming Jesus: Titular Christology in the Gospel of Mark.* JSNT Supplement Series 175. Sheffield, UK: Sheffield Academic Press, 1999. See p. 34.

———. *Prophet, Son, Messiah: Narrative Form and Function in Mark 14–16.* JSNT Supplement Series 97. Sheffield, UK: JSOT Press, 1994. See pp. 33–34.

———. *Teaching with Authority: Miracles and Christology in the Gospel of Mark.* JSNT Supplement Series 74. Sheffield, UK: Sheffield Academic Press, 1992. See pp. 31–32.

Bryan, Christopher. *A Preface to Mark: Notes on the Gospel in Its Literary and Cultural Settings*. Oxford/New York: Oxford University Press, 1993. See pp. 26–28.

Cahill, Michael. *The First Commentary on Mark: An Annotated Translation*. New York: Oxford University Press, 1998. See p. 85.

Camery-Hoggatt, Jerry. *Irony in Mark's Gospel: Text and subtext*. Society of New Testament Studies Monograph Series 72. Cambridge/New York: Cambridge University Press, 1992. See pp. 15–16.

Casey, Maurice. *Aramaic Sources of Mark's Gospel*. Society of New Testament Studies Monograph Series 102. Cambridge/New York: Cambridge University Press, 1998. See pp. 60–62.

Donahue, John R. *Hearing the Word of God: Reflections on the Sunday Readings: Year B*. Collegeville, MN: Liturgical Press, 2002. See p. 82.

———. "Windows and Mirrors: The Setting of Mark's Gospel." *Catholic Biblical Quarterly* 57 (1995): 1–26. See p. 51.

Donahue, John R. and Daniel J. Harrington. *The Gospel of Mark*. Sacra Pagina 2. Collegeville, MN: Liturgical Press, 2002. See p. 88.

Dowd, Sharon Echols. *Prayer, Power, and the Problem of Suffering: Mark 11:22–25 in the Context of Markan Theology*. Society of Biblical Literature Dissertation Series 105. Atlanta: Scholars Press, 1988. See pp. 43–44.

Dwyer, Timothy. *The Motif of Wonder in the Gospel of Mark*. JSNT Supplement Series 128. Sheffield, UK: Sheffield Academic Press, 1996. See pp. 45–47.

Enste, Stefan. *Kein Markustext in Qumran: Eine Untersuchung der These: Qumran-Fragment 7Q5 = Mk 6:52–53*. Novum Testamentum et Orbis Antiquus 45. Fribourg: Editions Universitaires; Göttingen: Vandenhoeck & Ruprecht, 1999. See pp. 66–67.

Fowler, Robert M. *Let the Reader Understand: Reader-Response Criticism and the Gospel of Mark*. Minneapolis: Fortress, 1991. See pp. 13–15.

Heil, John P. *The Gospel of Mark as a Model for Action: A Reader-Response Commentary*. Mahwah, NJ/New York: Paulist Press, 1992. See p. 86.

Hooker, Morna. *The Gospel According to Mark*. Black's New Testament Commentary. London: A & C Black, 1991; Peabody, MA: Hendrickson, 1992. See pp. 85–86.

Horsley, Richard A. *Hearing the Whole Story: The Politics of Plot in Mark's Gospel*. Louisville, KY: Westminster John Knox, 2001. See pp. 57–59.

Iersel, Bas van. *Reading Mark*. Collegeville, MN: Liturgical Press, 1988. See pp. 10–12.

Kee, Howard C. *The Community of the New Age: Studies in Mark's Gospel*. Philadelphia: Westminster, 1977. See p. 56.

Kelber, Werner. *The Kingdom in Mark: A New Place and New Time*. Philadelphia: Fortress, 1974. See pp. 55–56.

———. *Mark's Story of Jesus*. Philadelphia: Fortress, 1979. See pp. 55–56.

Kingsbury, Jack D. *Conflict in Mark: Jesus, Authorities, Disciples*. Minneapolis: Fortress, 1989. See pp. 20–22.

Kinukawa, Hisako. *Women and Jesus in Mark: A Japanese Feminist Perspective*. Maryknoll, NY: Orbis, 1994. See pp. 71–72.

LaVerdiere, Eugene. *The Beginning of the Gospel: Introducing the Gospel According to Mark*. Collegeville, MN: Liturgical Press, 1999. See p. 86.

Levine, Amy-Jill with M. Blickenstaff, eds. *A Feminist Companion to Mark*. Feminist Companion to the New Testament and Early Christian Writings 2. Sheffield, UK: Sheffield Academic Press, 2001. See p. 72.

Mack, Burton L. *A Myth of Innocence: Mark and Christian Origins*. Philadelphia: Fortress, 1988. See pp. 51–53.

Malbon, Elizabeth Struthers. *In the Company of Jesus: Characters in Mark's Gospel*. Louisville, KY: Westminster John Knox, 2000. See p. 23.

———. *Narrative Space and Mythic Meaning in Mark*. San Francisco: Harper & Row, 1988. See pp. 17–18.

Marcus, Joel. "The Jewish War and the *Sitz im Leben* of Mark." *Journal of Biblical Literature* 111 (1992): 441–462. See pp. 50–51.

———. *Mark 1–8*. Anchor Bible 27. New York: Doubleday, 2000. See pp. 86–87.

————. *The Way of the Lord: Christological Exegesis of the Old Testament in the Gospel of Mark*. Louisville, KY: Westminster John Knox, 1992. See pp. 34–36.

Marshall, Christopher D. *Faith as a Theme of Mark's Narrative*. Society of New Testament Studies Monograph Series 64. Cambridge/New York: Cambridge University Press, 1989. See pp. 44–45.

Matera, Frank J. *What Are They Saying About Mark?* Mahwah, NJ/New York: Paulist Press, 1987. See pp. 2, 4–7.

Mitchell, Joan. *Beyond Fear and Silence: A Feminist-Literary Reading of Mark*. New York: Continuum, 2001. See pp. 72–74.

Moloney, Francis J. *The Gospel of Mark: A Commentary*. Peabody, MA: Hendrickson, 2002. See pp. 87–88.

Myers, Ched. *Binding the Strong Man: A Political Reading of Mark's Story of Jesus*. Maryknoll, NY: Orbis, 1988. See pp. 56–57, 74–76.

O'Callaghan, Jose. "¿Papiros neotestamentarios en la cueva 7 de Qumran?" *Biblica* 53 (1972): 91–100. See pp. 64–65.

Oden, Thomas C. and Christopher A. Hall. *Mark*. Ancient Christian Commentary on Scripture 2. Downers Grove, IL: InterVarsity, 1998. See p. 85.

Peabody, David, Allan J. McNicol, and Lamar Cope. *One Gospel from Two: Mark's Use of Matthew and Luke*. Harrisburg, PA: Trinity Press, International. 2002. See pp. 62–64.

Peterson, Dwight N. *The Origins of Mark: The Markan Community in Current Debate*. Biblical Interpretation 48. Leiden: Brill, 2000. See pp. 55–57.

Pontifical Biblical Commission. *The Interpretation of the Bible in the Church*. Boston: St. Paul Books & Media, 1993. See pp. 1–2, 89.

Reiser, William. *Jesus in Solidarity with His People: A Theologian Looks at Mark*. Collegeville, MN: Liturgical Press, 2000. See pp. 79–81.

Schildgen, Brenda D. *Crisis and Continuity: Time in the Gospel of Mark*. JSNT Supplement Series 159. Sheffield, UK: Sheffield Academic Press, 1998. See pp. 18–20.

Schneck, Richard. *Isaiah in the Gospel of Mark I–VIII*. BIBAL Dissertation Series 1. Vallejo, CA: BIBAL Press, 1994. See pp. 36–37.

Selvidge, Marla J. *Woman, Cult, and Miracle Recital: A Redactional Critical Investigation on Mark 5:24–34*. Lewisburg, PA: Bucknell University Press, 1990. See pp. 70–71.

Shiner, Whitney T. *Follow Me! Disciples in Markan Rhetoric*. Society of Biblical Literature Dissertation Series 145. Atlanta: Scholars Press, 1995. See pp. 39–40.

Sweetland, Dennis M. *Our Journey with Jesus: Discipleship according to Mark*. Wilmington, DE: Glazier, 1987. See pp. 37–39.

Taylor, Vincent. *The Gospel According to Mark*. London: Macmillan, 1952; 2nd ed., 1966. See p. 85.

Telford, William R. *The Theology of the Gospel of Mark*. New Testament Theology. Cambridge/New York: Cambridge University Press, 1999. See pp. 29–31.

———, ed. *The Interpretation of Mark*. Studies in New Testament Interpretation; 2nd ed. Edinburgh: T & T Clark, 1995. See p. 31.

Thiede, Carsten P. *The Earliest Gospel Manuscript? The Qumran Papyrus 7Q5 and Its Significance for New Testament Studies*. Exeter, UK: Paternoster, 1992. See pp. 65–66.

Thurston, Bonnie B. *Preaching Mark*. Minneapolis: Fortress, 2002. See p. 82.

Tolbert, Mary Ann. *Sowing the Gospel: Mark's World in Literary-Historical Perspective*. Minneapolis: Fortress, 1989. See pp. 24–26.

Trainor, Michael F. *The Quest for Home: The Household in Mark's Community*. Collegeville, MN: Liturgical Press, 2001. See pp. 40–42.

Waetjen, Herman C. *A Reordering of Power: A Sociopolitical Reading of Mark's Gospel*. Minneapolis: Fortress, 1989. See pp. 76–78.

Watts, Rikki. *Isaiah's New Exodus and Mark*. Wissenschaftliche Untersuchungen zum Neuen Testament 2/88. Tübingen: Mohr Siebeck, 1997; Grand Rapids: Baker, 2000. See p. 37.

Williams, Joel F. *Other Followers of Jesus: Minor Characters as Major Figures in Mark's Gospel*. JSNT Supplement Series 102. Sheffield, UK: Sheffield Academic Press, 1994. See pp. 22–23.

Wills, Lawrence M. *The Quest of the Historical Gospel: Mark, John, and the Origins of the Gospel Genre*. London/New York: Routledge, 1997. See pp. 59–60.

Yarbro Collins, Adela. *The Beginnings of the Gospel: Probings of Mark in Context*. Minneapolis: Fortress, 1992. See pp. 53–55.

Other Books in This Series

Other Books in This Series

What are they saying about Paul and the Law?
  by Veronica Koperski

What are they saying about the Pastoral Epistles?
  by Mark Harding

What are they saying about Catholic Ethical Method?
  by Todd A. Salzman

What are they saying about New Testament Apocalyptic?
  by Scott M. Lewis, S.J.

What are they saying about Environmental Theology?
  by John Hart

What are they saying about the Catholic Epistles?
  by Philip B. Harner